SAINTS WHO
SPOKE ENGLISH

SAINTS WHO SPOKE ENGLISH

BY LEO KNOWLES

CARILLON BOOKS
St. Paul, Minnesota

SAINTS WHO SPOKE ENGLISH
A Carillon Book

Carillon Books Edition published 1979

ISBN: 0-89310-045-5 (Hardcover)
0-89310-046-3 (Paperback)

Library of Congress Catalog Card Number 78-74329

Carillon Books
2115 Summit Avenue
St. Paul, Minnesota 55105 U.S.A.

Some of the material in this book on St. Thomas More, St. Edmund Campion and St. Philip Howard appeared originally in *Catholic Digest*. I am obliged to the Managing Editor, Mr. Richard Reece, for permission to reprint it here.

L.K.

CONTENTS

vii

1

In Wild Northumbria

As soon as the lone horseman appeared out of the morning mists, Lilla suspected treachery. A sharp eye and a shrewd brain had earned him his job as the King's chief minister, and he sensed at once that this stranger from the opposite end of England was not what he pretended to be.

True, the fellow was civil enough. What was more, he had brought handsome gifts: a cloak with a bronze clasp for King Edwin and a jewelled brooch for the Queen.

In his soft dialect he explained that his name was Eumer and that he had an important message to deliver from Cuichelm, King of Wessex.

"What is this message?" Lilla asked cautiously. "I must give it directly to your King," replied the ambassador, his eyes narrowing. "Those are my master's orders. Nobody but the King of Northumbria must hear what I have to say."

Inside the rough stone palace beside the River Derwent, Edwin was pacing up and down among the rushes which strewed the floor of his throne-room. Every inch a

1

king, he looked as tense and anxious as any other expec-
tant father, for the long-awaited moment had almost
come. Instead of going to Mass this Easter Sunday morning, Ethelberga, his young Christian Queen, had gone
into labor. It was their first child and the midwives had
predicted that her confinement would be long and difficult.

Told of Eumer's arrival, Edwin made an impatient ges-
ture. For a moment, Lilla half-hoped that he would refuse to meet the ambassador from Wessex. The hope
passed swiftly, for the minister well knew that to slight a
monarch who had always been neutral, if not actually
friendly, would be foolish. Edwin had enemies enough
without making fresh ones.

Minutes later the King had settled himself in the raised
chair which served him as a throne, his ministers and
bodyguard ranged formally around him. From the bed-
chamber within came purposeful, bustling sounds as the
midwives murmured encouragement to their royal pa-
tient. Back into Edwin's mind came the question which
had lately troubled him insistently. Would the sacrifices
of his own pagan priests or the prayers of Paulinus, the
Christian bishop, bring his wife safely through her
ordeal? And if she did come through, how would he
know which God or gods should receive thanks?

Another moment and the wiry little ambassador was
bowing before him. As he returned the salute, Edwin
found himself wondering, for the first time, what on earth
King Cuichelm could want with him.

"May I speak with your majesty alone?"

The request, violating all known custom, brought
Edwin up with a start. Lifting his great head, with its
beard and mane of fair hair, he stared at the visitor with
eyes of piercing blue.

"Speak with me alone?" he roared. "That you may not. Each man here is my trusted servant. You must say what you have to say in front of them all."

Eumer licked his lips nervously and glanced round. To Lilla it seemed that he was gauging the distance between himself and all of them.

Taking a step forward, Eumer reached inside his jerkin.

"Then allow me, Sir, to show you this," he said.

Even before he saw the knife, Lilla realised what he must do. A thin shaft of sunlight caught the raised steel, but already the minister had flung himself across the King's unprotected body. When the blade fell, it was Lilla who caught it full in the chest. Within seconds he was dead, poisoned by the deadly venom which coated it.

Small Eumer may have been, but in the terrible struggle which followed he fought with a giant's strength. A second man, a bodyguard named Forthhere, fell victim to the poisoned dagger before the assassin's corpse, run through by half a dozen swords, was dragged from the throne-room and thrown into the cesspit outside.

Gazing sadly upon the lifeless body of his minister, Edwin tried to find answers to the questions which now raced through his mind. Why had Cuichelm wanted to kill him? What manner of man was this Eumer, who had travelled for many days to carry out the murder, knowing that a violent death would be his only reward? Most important of all, by whose power had his own life been preserved? Had the pagan gods intervened to save him, or his wife's God, the God of the Christians?

That some supernatural agency was looking after him, Edwin had long been aware. Indeed, he had been assured of it in a remarkable way.

Years before, when his enemy Ethelfrid reigned in Northumbria, the young prince had found shelter with Redwald, King of East Anglia. His host had promised to protect him, but when Ethelfrid dangled a fat bribe under his nose and threatened to declare war if he did not take it, Redwald decided that it was an offer which he could not refuse. He agreed to kill Edwin or at least to deliver him to Ethelfrid's henchmen.

Warned by a friend of the danger which threatened him, Edwin went out into the night and sat on a stone to brood over his fate. No use to run away; he would be caught within hours. Even if he did get beyond the borders of East Anglia, where else could he hope to hide? Years on the run had made him a marked man. Now he was at the end, caught like a rabbit in a trap.

Dejected, Edwin glanced up at the starlit sky and found that he was not alone. A stranger, tall and kindly-looking, stood gazing down at him.

"Why are you out here alone when everyone else is in bed?" the man asked.

"What is that to you?" Edwin retorted. The man's smile irritated him.

"Very well, you don't need to tell me," the stranger replied calmly. "I know all about the danger you are in. But answer me this. What would you do for the person who could save you?"

"Why, anything—anything in the world," replied Edwin, astonished not so much by the question as by the way in which it was asked.

"And if, in the future, that man should give you advice about your whole life, both in this world and in the next, would you not want to follow it?"

"Yes. Yes, of course I would." Edwin was even more bewildered, but somehow his heart felt suddenly lighter.

The stranger laid a hand on his head.

"Remember this conversation, and this sign, in years to come," he said, "and perform what you have promised."

Then he was gone, suddenly and completely, as though he had melted into the night air.

Edwin was still sitting on the stone, trying to decide whether it had all really happened, when the friend who had warned him earlier came running out with a face covered in smiles.

"Redwald has relented," he shouted gleefully. "When he told the Queen that he was going to do Ethelfrid's dirty work, she said it was a downright disgrace and that if he let himself be bullied into such an act of treachery he'd never be able to hold his head up again. In the end he gave way and promised her that instead of doing away with you he'd stand up to that tyrant Ethelfrid."

In the battle that followed Ethelfrid was killed and the young exile found himself ruler of a kingdom which covered a large part of Northern England and Southern Scotland.

Shortly afterwards, in the year 625, Edwin sent ambassadors south to ask Eadbald, King of Kent, for his sister's hand in marriage. Stiffly Eadbald replied that as a Christian he could not marry his sister to any pagan monarch, since her faith might then suffer.

Edwin assured him that Ethelberga would be perfectly free, as his wife, to continue practising her religion, and he readily agreed Paulinus, newly ordained as a bishop, should live at the court and look after her spiritual welfare. So, with much feasting and rejoicing, the wedding went ahead.

Politics, rather than romance, had dictated Edwin's choice of a bride. An alliance with Kent could be useful, especially if any neighboring king should attack him. Like many another arranged marriage, this one turned out to be extremely happy. Edwin loved his young wife

dearly and he was overjoyed when, in the evening of that
eventful Easter Day, Paulinus announced to him that he
was the father of a baby daughter.

"And the Queen?" asked Edwin anxiously.

"She is well, Sir," replied Paulinus with a smile. "At
this moment her maids are making her ready to receive
you."

Later that night, after he had thanked his own gods,
Edwin listened as Paulinus gave thanks to the Father,
the Son and the Holy Spirit. As the bishop went on to
thank Mary, the Mother of Christ, for her intercession,
Edwin felt more strongly than ever that here, and not in
the tawdry ceremonies of the pagan temples, was where
the truth lay.

Ever since his marriage Edwin had been increasingly
drawn towards Christianity. Indeed he had promised
King Eadbald, his brother-in-law, that he would embrace
it if he found it to be the true religion. Now he readily
agreed that his daughter should be baptised and on the
following Pentecost Sunday the little girl became
Northumbria's first native-born Christian.

Yet Edwin did not accept baptism for himself. Though
a strong king and a brave warrior, he was by nature a
deeply reflective man who weighed his decisions carefully. The years of exile and danger, when any wrong
move could have been fatal, had added greatly to his
natural caution. Before taking the plunge, he resolved to
put God through one final test. If he were granted victory over Cuichelm and his enemies in Wessex, he would
become a Christian.

God came through with flying colors: Edwin's
would-be murderers were well and truly thrashed. Yet
despite the undertaking, Edwin still could not bring
himself to part with paganism. From far-off Rome Pope
Boniface had been following events in Northumbria with

eager interest. Realising that Edwin was dithering on the threshold of the Church, he pressed him to enter without further delay. "How guilty are people who hang on to their idols and their miserable superstitions!" wrote the Pope. "Idols have eyes and do not see, they have ears and do not hear, noses and do not smell, hands and do not feel, feet and do not walk. . . . Though we have tried hard to understand why you cling to your belief in these home-made gods, we remain bewildered that you should be so deceived."

For Ethelberga, too, there was a letter urging her to do everything within her power to encourage her husband's conversion. With it came two charming presents: a silver looking-glass and an ivory comb.

It was Paulinus, of course, who kept the Pope informed of the King's zigzag progress toward Christianity. The bishop had himself come from Rome as one of the second wave of missionaries whom Pope Gregory the Great had sent to Kent in the wake of St. Augustine. From the outset both his personality and his preaching had impressed Edwin deeply. Though the Roman Empire had now crumbled, Edwin sensed the shadow of its former glory in this dignified, black-bearded man with his slight stoop and his piercing eyes.

One day, soon after he had received the Pope's letter, Edwin sat meditating alone, just as he had done on that night at the court of King Redwald when his life was so suddenly and so miraculously spared. Once again he looked up. This time it was Paulinus who stood beside him.

"Do you recognise this sign?" asked the Bishop. Gently he laid his hand on Edwin's head.

The King started up, astonished. He had told no-one of the stranger's message, not even his wife. Not knowing what it meant, he had always been half-afraid to speak of it. Sometimes, indeed, he still wondered whether the stranger's visit had really happened, or whether, exhausted and in despair, he had fallen into a feverish sleep and dreamed the whole thing.

Now he knew the truth, knew from Whom the message had come, understood its meaning. Trembling, he tried to fall on his knees in front of Paulinus. With a swift movement the Bishop raised him to his feet. Reminding him of all that God had done for him, he begged him not to delay his conversion any longer.

Not only did Edwin agree to be baptised; he decided straight away that he must do his utmost to bring his friends and advisers—including the pagan priests into the Church with him. He did not, however, use kingly coercion. Instead he called a meeting so that the claims of Christianity could be compared with the religion of their forefathers.

The first to speak was the chief priest, Coifi, who now revealed that he, too, had become increasingly disillusioned with his gods. For, as he pointed out to Edwin: "Nobody has spent more time and energy in worshipping them than I, and yet there are many of your subjects who receive far greater favors from you than ever I have done. They get on in life and I don't.

"Now if the gods were good for anything, surely they would look after me better than this! So if we find that Christianity offers a better deal, I suggest that we accept it without delay."

A more thoughtful, and certainly more disinterested, contribution came from an elderly minister whose name we have, unfortunately, not been told.

"It seems to me, Sir," he told Edwin, "that this life of ours is like the swift flight of a sparrow through the hall where you sit at supper with us on a winter night. Outside there is rain and snow, but we have a good fire, and while he is with us the sparrow is safe from the storm. Yet in no time he flies out again into the cold and the darkness, and we see him no more.

"Our life is, like the sparrow's journey, pathetically brief. Of what comes before it, or what follows afterwards, we know nothing at all. If this new doctrine can teach us, then surely it deserves to be followed."

Vivid words! Even after so many centuries, the old man's simile springs living from the page; often since that far-off day it has been quoted and praised. Upon those who heard him speak, his speech made a profound impact.

Straight away, at Coifi's request, Paulinus was called in to preach to them. So powerful were his words that the old priest, after a lifetime of pagan worship, demanded there and then that they should turn their backs on the discredited gods and set fire to their temples.

The law decreed that no priest could bear arms or ride any beast but a mare. Now an astonished populace watched as Coifi, mounted by royal permission on the King's own stallion, rode purposefully through the town toward the main temple. Halting outside the door, he deliberately flung a spear through it, profaning the spot for all time.

Now the people were convinced: Coifi had gone mad. There was, however, an even greater shock in store. For next junior priests and servants appeared with blazing torches, and soon the flames of the burning temple rose high above the town.

Edwin had been saved from death, and his child born, on Easter Sunday. It was on Easter Sunday one year later, in 627, that the King and a host of his subjects, were baptised by Paulinus at York. Soon afterwards the King built a church on the spot where he had become a Christian. Today it is the site of York Minster, one of England's

greatest cathedrals, visited each year by visitors from the
United States and from all over the world.

Among the Northumbrians who received Baptism that
day was a girl named Hilda, daughter of the King's
nephew Hereric. When she became a Christian, the
young princess was thirteen.

It was later said that, just before Hilda was born and
while her father was in exile, her mother had a dream in
which she searched for her husband desperately and in
vain. In fact the poor woman never did see Hereric
again, for he was poisoned by his enemies. In the dream,
however, she looked underneath her robe and discovered a jewel so bright that its light shone throughout.
Britain.

Of course we do not have to believe the story. In a
world of pagans eager for signs and wonders, Christian
teachers were no doubt ready to retail pious legends
without examining them too critically. Nevertheless,
Hilda did grow up to be a very remarkable young woman
indeed.

In those days nobody, inside or outside the Church,
campaigned for women's rights, and the very suggestion
that women should be ordained as priests would have
brought screams of horror from every corner of Christendom. Yet young Hilda was to play a huge part in building
up the Church in Britain and she is undoubtedly one of
its greatest saints. To this day, hundreds of churches
throughout England are dedicated to her.

When we meet her again she is 33 and setting out for
France to join her sister, who is already a nun at a convent near Paris. We have no detailed information about
her life during the previous twenty years; quite possibly
she had married and lost her husband while she was still
young, for it seems unlikely that a lady of those days—

and a princess to boot—would have remained single in
the world for so long.

We do know that they were extremely turbulent years,
for Hilda and for all her fellow-Northumbrians. After a
seventeen-year reign, Edwin had died in a battle against
two neighbouring monarchs and for a time the kingdom
had lapsed once more into paganism.

By the time Oswald, a devout Christian, became King,
Paulinus had gone back to Kent. When Oswald sought a
new Bishop for Northumbria he did not, however, look to
the Christian kingdom in the South. Instead he looked
North, to the great monastery which the Irish St. Co-
lumba had founded on the island of Iona off the West
coast of Scotland.

Like other Christians in those parts the Iona monks
belonged to the Celtic Church, which had long been cut
off from contact with Rome. The Celtic Christians domi-
nated, not only Scotland, but also Ireland, Wales, Devon,
Cornwall and Brittany. Though sound on fundamentals
and often extremely holy, they had, during the years of
separation, developed certain practices of their own to
which they clung with great tenacity. In particular they
administered Baptism in a manner different from that
followed by the rest of the Church and they kept Easter
at a different time. Their monks, in place of the circular
Roman tonsure, drew an imaginary line from ear to ear
across the crown and shaved off all the hair in front of it.

Though to us these differences may seem less than
vital, to our forebears they loomed large. In Northumbria
the two traditions collided. Having been taught Roman
customs by Paulinus, the Christians there now found
themselves part of the Celtic Church, with a dynamic
Irishman named Aidan as their Bishop.

How Hilda felt about the clash of customs, once again

we have no means of knowing. She could not have been
an immediate convert to Celtic ways, otherwise she
would hardly have headed for a convent in France.

As it turned out, she never arrived there. She was in
East Anglia, waiting for a boat, when a message arrived
from Bishop Aidan. Would she please return home and
take charge of a new convent which he was setting up
beside the River Wear? So Hilda headed back to Northumbria and began her monastic career at the place which
is now called South Shields, moving later to another convent at West Hartlepool, further along England's North-
east coast.

Like many another saint, Aidan was a shrewd judge of
people. He had been sent to Northumbria after the first
monk chosen had antagonised the already-bewildered
natives by ramming the Gospel down their throats with
hell-fire ferocity. Back at Iona, Aidan told him where he
had gone wrong.

"You should have fed them the milk of doctrine gently,
just as new-born babies are fed," he said. Whereupon
Aidan found himself unanimously chosen to go back to
the new mission in place of his colleague.

Plainly the canny Irishman had decided that Hilda
was too fine a woman to lose to a convent abroad. Possibly he set up the South Shields convent with the express
object of attracting her back. From now on she stayed
firmly put in her native kingdom and totally committed
to Christianity in its Celtic form.

Outside the convent walls, the battles between
neighbouring kings continued, as England struggled
painfully toward nationhood. Having reigned for nine
years, Oswald was killed in a war with Penda of Mercia,
one of the enemies who had done away with Edwin.
Like his predecessor, the pious Oswald was immediately

venerated as a saint and many were the miraculous cures attributed to him.

Even though he had now caused the death of two Christian kings, Penda seems to have had more than a sneaking regard for their religion. When large numbers of his subjects, including his own son, chose Baptism, he made no objection. Indeed he actually sneered at those who did not keep up the practice of their new Faith. "They are miserable wretches if they won't serve the God in whom they believe!" he snorted.

No doubt Penda felt that, his own gods having so far given complete satisfaction, there was no need for him to change his allegiance. However, his third clash with Northumbria was to be the unlucky one. In a battle with Oswald's successor, his brother Oswy, the pagan king was killed and his army routed. Penda of Mercia would trouble Northumbria no more.

In thanksgiving for his victory, Oswy decided to donate land for twelve new religious houses, one of them to be situated at Whitby. So once again, at Oswy's request, Hilda moved south along the coast. It was to be the last and most important move of her life.

Along with his gift of land, Oswy presented something far more precious. His little daughter, then barely a year old, was brought to Whitby to grow up under Hilda's careful eye and, in due time, to become a nun.

To commit a child in this way may seem, to our minds, strange and even repugnant. Seventh-century Christians saw things differently. Asked to become foster-mother to the little princess, Hilda accepted joyfully. Everything worked out happily, for not only did the child, Aelfled, grow up to be a nun; she succeeded her foster-mother as abbess of the great monastery which Hilda now founded.

Today Whitby is just a little Yorkshire fishing-port.

Hilda's great abbey, its buildings long vanished, is a
paragraph in the history books. Yet here was one of
Christian Europe's mighty powerhouses and Hilda was
the dynamo that drove it.

She ruled, not only a convent of women, but a monastery of men—a state of affairs which, once again, seems
strange and even bizarre to us. Yet double foundations of
this kind were once common from Ireland to Egypt.

In earlier times Christians of both sexes sometimes
lived a brother-and-sister existence in a sort of commune.
St. Augustine of Hippo, as a young man, belonged to one
of these. The dangers were obvious, however, and the
communes soon gave way to properly-regulated monasteries built side by side.

Where the abbess was the Superior she had spiritual
charge of priests and even Bishops; St. Brigid, in Ireland,
wielded this overall jurisdiction and Hilda's powers
were just as wide. Like Brigid's, her influence extended
far beyond the monastery walls, for in those days, in the
Celtic world at least, there was no parish structure. It was
in the monasteries that priests were trained and from the
monasteries that they went out to evangelise the countryside.

Hilda gave supreme importance to study, and especially the study of the Scriptures. So effective was her
training program that no fewer than five of her monks
were ordained as Bishops. One of these, John of Beverley, himself became a saint of considerable renown.

Meanwhile, the conflict between Romanisers and
Celts was moving rapidly towards a confrontation, thanks
chiefly to the efforts of Wilfrid, a holy but somewhat can-
tankerous son of Northumbria who had recently returned
to his native kingdom from abroad. Wilfrid had begun his
ecclesiastical career as a monk in Aidan's monastery at
Lindisfarne, the "Holy Island" off the Northumbrian

coast. Under the influence of Queen Eanfleda, who had
befriended him when he was a court page-boy, he
quickly decided that Roman customs were right and Celtic customs wrong. After years spent in France and
Rome, he was now busily engaged in trying to bring his
countrymen into line.

King Oswy himself must often have wished that the
differences could be resolved. His wife, Eanfleda, was
Edwin's daughter; after her father's death she had been
brought up in Kent. Her insistence on following the
Roman observance meant that, while one half of the
court was celebrating Easter, the other half was still in
Lent! Prompted by Wilfrid, the King decided to end the
confusion once and for all.

In the year 663 or 664 (we are not sure which) Oswy
called a meeting to settle the issue once and for all.
Whitby was chosen as the venue. After listening to arguments from both sides, the King, in a famous judgement,
came down on the side of Rome and St. Peter.

"I will not oppose this Keeper of the Gates of
Heaven," he declared. "Instead I will obey his com-
mands as faithfully as I can. If I don't, he might shut
those gates against me!"

Defeated, most of the Celtic monks and nuns departed
for Ireland and Scotland, leaving Northumbria to the
Roman party. Hilda did not join them. Instead she submitted to the Synod's judgement, though with a heavy
heart; for throughout the discussions she had argued vigorously that her beloved native Church should retain its
own identity.

What her motives were we can only guess, but we may
be sure that they went deeper than Easter calculations
and the shape of monks' tonsures. The Celtic Church
was, as we have seen, a monastic Church. Its monasteries
were places of real, sometimes extreme, asceticism.

Even where the rule was less severe, as we may be sure
it was at Whitby, the monks and nuns fasted regularly
and devoted long hours to study and prayer. Their kindness to Christian and pagan alike made them greatly
loved.

There were, to be sure, splendid monasteries outside
the Celtic world where all these virtues were practised.
However, Hilda had almost certainly heard stories about
the other kind: so-called convents which were in truth
nothing more than hostels for unmarried daughters,
where the nuns wore jewellery and cosmetics, tunics and
hoods of fine linen sewn with ribbons and colored scarlet, purple or blue; where fancy hair-styles were all the
rage and fingernails grown long and curved, like hawks'
talons. The description comes from St. Aldhelm, a
monk-Bishop from Wessex who was Hilda's contemporary and we can imagine how Hilda and her friends must
have shuddered at the thought of their own world being
touched by a similar corruption.

At the Synod of Whitby, then, the Celtic Christians
were fighting, not merely for their customs, but for a way
of life which had brought Christ to countless pagans and
which had already produced many great saints. To sub-
mit to Rome must indeed have seemed like a betrayal of
their highest ideals.

Wisely, Rome made no move to condemn those who
found it impossible to obey. Time would eventually
bring the wayward sheep back to the fold.

So much, then, for Hilda's achievements and for the
part which she played at a critical moment in the
Church's history. But, you may now be asking, what was
she really *like*?

St. Bede, who is virtually our only source, has left
scarcely any of the intimate, human details that would
bring her to life for us. He says only that kings and

princes frequently brought their problems to her and that all who knew her instinctively called her "Mother."

Her most famous protegé is not to be found among the Bishops whom she trained, nor among the Kings whom she advised. He was a poor stable-hand, a layman who worked for the monastery. His name was Caedmon.

For most of his life Caedmon had a social hang-up which caused him much distress. Though he enjoyed convivial evenings in the ale-house, he found himself totally unable to take part in the singing which often formed part of the evening's entertainment. When the harp was passed round and his friends, amid roars of approval, improvised their songs, Caedmon would slink out into the night. Not only could he not sing; when it came to inprovisation he did not have an idea in his head.

One evening, as the ale flowed and the dreaded harp once more bore down on him, Caedmon got up to make his usual shame-faced exit.

"Where are you off to, then, Caedmon?" called one of the more inebriated members of the company.

"Got to go and see to the horses," muttered Caedmon. As he shuffled out, a gale of laughter followed him. By now everyone knew about Caedmon's problem.

As it happened he *did* have to see to the horses, for it was his turn to guard them all night. When he had seen that all was secure, he lay down to sleep in the straw.

"Caedmon, sing a song for me." Caedmon started, blinking up in the darkness. Who had spoken? How had he got into the stable.

The man who stood before him was a stranger. Caedmon, despite the gloom, could see his face clearly and knew at once that he was no robber. But who was he?

"Sing, Caedmon." The voice was kind, yet insistent.

"I can't," murmured Caedmon, bewildered. "That's why I left the ale-house early and came on here."

"All the same, you are going to sing for me now."

"But what shall I sing?" asked Caedmon, more bewildered than ever.

"Sing about Creation, about the beginning of all things."

And sing Caedmon did. To his own astonishment, to his total disbelief, he sang a song which neither he nor anyone else had ever heard before, a song perfect in metre and of an elegance which certainly surpassed anything ever heard in the ale-house. Here it is in modern English:

It is well for us to worship the Guardian of Heaven,
The might of the Creator and the power of His mind.
When Eternal God began His work
He first made Heaven as a roof for Earth's children
Then the World-warden made Earth itself,
Land for men to live on, Almighty Lord!

As Bede himself observes, no translation can do justice to the original.

Caedmon was already middle-aged, but at Hilda's suggestion, he now became one of her monks. Inside the monastery, large portions of Scripture were especially translated into Northumbrian and on these the former stable-hand exercised his new-found gift. At Caedmon's dictation his brethren wrote down long poems based on the books of Genesis and Exodus.

As a monk Caedmon became holy and much loved; in some parts of Britain he was later honored as a saint. The account of his death is one of the best things in Bede's great *Ecclesiastical History of the English Nation.*

During the last six years of her own life Hilda suffered severe ill-health. This she bore cheerfully and went on working just as she had always done. "We ought to thank

God just as much when we are ill as we do when we are well," she told her charges.

She died at dawn on November 17, 680, having first received Holy Communion and begged those around her to preserve peace among themselves. She was not at her beloved Whitby but at Hackness, another monastery which she had founded some distance away. When monks arrived at Whitby with the news, they found the community there already reciting prayers for the dead. The monastery bell, tolling of its own accord, had announced Hilda's passing; and one nun had seen, in a vision, Hilda's soul accompanied to Heaven by angels.

For two centuries the Whitby monastery flourished, until the pagan Vikings swept down to destroy it, as they destroyed so many of the other great monasteries around the coasts of the British Isles. For the Celtic Church it was a death-blow: even before the Norman conquerors arrived, full of orthodox zeal, most of the Celtic survivors had submitted to Rome. Before the eleventh century was over, the submission was complete.

2

Britain's Wonder-Worker

Everyone watching from the shore could see that the monks were in terrible danger. In five rafts they had brought timber down the River Tyne for the new monastery which they were building at the river-mouth. They had almost reached the landing-stage when a fierce current, snatching each raft like a beast of prey, carried all five out to sea.

The monks' oars were useless against the waves which already washed angrily over the rough, heavily-laden craft. Plainly it could not be long before monks and cargo were lost in the cold waters of the North Sea.

Their ordeal won little sympathy from the spectators, most of whom were watching their struggles with cruel enjoyment.

"Serve them right, the psalm-singing fools," jeered a brutish-looking herdsman. "What do they want to come here for anyway, disturbing our ways and upsetting our gods?"

A chorus of jeers applauded his words. At the same time sidelong glances were cast at the broad-shouldered young man who stood, a little taller than the rest, watching his brethren fight their losing battle with the waves.

In their desperate plight the victims were too preoccupied to heed the taunts. Indeed, they were now so far out to sea that they could scarcely hear them. It was at himself that the jeers were really directed, Cuthbert well knew that. Yet, for the moment at least, he ignored them. Only his lips moved as he prayed silently for the tiny figures who were now clinging helplessly to the tossing rafts.

Around him the hoots and shouts grew louder and more excited. Only a few minutes more, surely, and the monks must drown!

Finally Cuthbert spoke. His voice, though calm, rang clearly above those of the pagan rabble around him. Some of them, he well knew, were officially Christians; but pagans at heart they remained.

"Instead of jeering at those unfortunate men," said Cuthbert gravely, "why not be kind and pray for their rescue?"

For a moment there was silence. Even the roaring of the waves seemed to fade to a whisper. In the end it was the herdsman who faced him, mouth twisted in an ugly sneer.

"You think that praying is going to save them?" he demanded.

"I know that God will show mercy if only we ask," replied Cuthbert calmly.

The herdsman turned to the crowd.

"You hear that, everybody?" he yelled. "He says he can rescue his pals out there, without even getting his feet wet!"

Ignoring the fresh roars of laughter which greeted this sally, Cuthbert knelt down. Aloud, in front of them all, he prayed that God would bring the drowning monks safely to shore.

Slowly, unbelievably, the rafts turned. To gasps of astonishment from the crowd, they ploughed sedately through the waves toward the mouth of the river.

On the landing-stage a joyful welcome greeted the survivors and then the work of unloading the timber began. Monks do not regard even a miracle as an excuse for not getting on with the business in hand.

Slowly the pagans began to shuffle away, their faces a mixture of shock and bewilderment. Who was this Cuthbert, who could command the wind and the waves? Evidently some kind of magician, and a powerful one at that. Better not get the wrong side of him, or something very nasty indeed might happen!

Cuthbert, reading their thoughts, smiled as he watched them go.

"Don't imagine I did it myself," he called after them. "God, the true God, answered my prayer. And he'll answer yours if you'll only give Him a chance."

Once the monastery got established and the monks began their work in the countryside, most of these people would accept the Gospel; of that Cuthbert was confident. Already, in other parts of Northumbria, the simple Celtic monks had made themselves greatly loved. It was not their preaching alone which made such a profound impression. Anyone in need soon learned that the monks were always ready to help. They fed the poor, cared for the sick, prayed with the dying, always had a kind word for the children. It was hardly surprising that men and women as well as the youngsters, would come forward eagerly to greet a passing Brother, to touch his hand or to get a blessing. And soon he, Cuthbert, would be one of their number.

Of all the missionaries who carried the Faith through
Britain in those days, Cuthbert is probably the best
known and the best loved. Whereas Hilda is a shadowy
figure, Cuthbert can be seen clearly across the centuries.
For this we have to thank Bede, who this time generously
left us a whole biography, and an anonymous monk who
also wrote Cuthbert's life-story soon after his death.

Curthbert was born around the year 634, somewhere
near what is now the English-Scottish border. Who his
parents were we do not know; like other well-born
youngsters of his time Cuthbert was fostered out when
he was still very small. Of his foster-mother we are told
only that she was a widow and that her name was
Kenswith.

Young Cuthbert was an exceptionally fit and agile lad
who could out-jump, out-run and out-wrestle even those
older and bigger than he was. Happiness meant doing
just that, until a strange incident brought him up with a
sharp jolt and altered the whole course of his life.

At the age of eight he was playing one day with a group
of other boys when a little lad who was only three suddenly broke off and burst into tears. At first nobody could
find out what was wrong.

"Oh, Cuthbert," he sobbed finally, as the others stared
in amazement, "how can you waste your time in these
stupid games when God wants you to be a priest and a
Bishop when you grow up?"

Cuthbert put his arm round the tiny prophet and dried
his tears. Then he went home.

From now on he was a different Cuthbert, the biggest
difference being that the time spent in play was now
largely spent in prayer, for himself and for other people.
At the same time he remained friendly, cheerful and
physically fit—as he needed to be for the tough life
which lay ahead.

Too young to enter a monastery, Cuthbert went to work as a shepherd-boy on the bleak Border fells. During this period he had a number of experiences which his saintly biographers firmly believed to be supernatural in origin. About some of these, I must confess, I have my doubts.

On one occasion, for example, Cuthbert developed a nasty swelling in his knee, which gave him much pain and left him lame. A kindly stranger, passing his home, treated the afflicted knee with a poultice of hot flour and water, then mounted his horse and rode on his way.

Within a few days the knee was cured. This, coupled with the stranger's handsome appearance and white robes, convinced Cuthbert that his physician was no passing folk-healer but none other than the Archangel Raphael—he who was sent by God to cure the eyesight of Tobit. For sceptics like myself, biographer Bede has this stern warning: "If anyone think it incredible that an angel appear on horseback, let him read the history of the Maccabees, in which angels are said to have come on horseback to the assistance of Judas Maccabaeus, and to defend God's own temple!"

Despite these signs of divine favor, Cuthbert was in his teens before he finally decided to become a monk. His mind seems to have been made up by a piece of good fortune, also given miraculous status, which occurred as he was travelling far from home one cold winter Friday.

Like other devout Christians, Cuthbert practiced the regular Friday habit of fasting until evening. For this reason he refused to accept food from a kind lady in whose house he sheltered, though he allowed her to feed his horse before continuing on his way.

At nightfall he found some deserted huts on the fells and, having got hold of some hay for the horse, prepared himself for a long, hungry rest. The horse, having

had his hay, began to nibble at the roof-thatch, when
to Cuthbert's astonishment a package wrapped in a
linen cloth fell from the thatch on to the floor in front
of him.

Cuthbert unwrapped it—and found a still-warm loaf
and some meat! Reasonably, in the circumstances, he
took the food to be manna from Heaven and made short
work of it. I just hope that some hungry shepherd did not
come by next day and find his lunch gone!

The monastery which he finally entered was Melrose,
beside the River Tweed, a foundation closely connected
with Lindisfarne. Here he trained under the Abbot, St.
Boisil, who greeted the new postulant with the words:
"Here, for sure, is a true servant of the Lord! "

Throughout his life Cuthbert had the way ahead
pointed out by prophecy. Later, when he lay seriously ill,
Boisil foretold Cuthbert's future as a Bishop. Cuthbert,
who wanted only to be a humble monk, was not at all
happy at the news.

At Melrose, and later at Lindisfarne, he developed a
reputation for asceticism. On sleep, especially, he made
constant war, sometimes staying up on three nights out of
four so that he could devote the time to prayer and work
for others.

"If anyone wakes me in the middle of the night," he
remarked once, "I am never in the least annoyed. Instead I get up straight away and begin to think of something useful."

When he was staying anywhere near the sea he would
often go down to the seashore and wade into the icy
waters until they reached his chin. There he would
spend hours, chanting the psalms.

He took great pains to conceal these nocturnal trips,
but one night an inquisitive monk followed him and remained hidden while Cuthbert carried out his devotions.

When the saint finally came dripping wet from the water, the astonished spectator saw two animals—the monk thought that they were otters but they were probably seals—follow him and dry him by rubbing him with their bodies.

Like St. Francis, Cuthbert was always a friend to animals and a keen observer of their ways. It was typical of him that on his Friday journey he showed more concern for his horse than for himself. Later, on a missionary expedition through the Northumbrian wilds, he and his young companion found themselves far from any human dwelling and faint from lack of food. Suddenly a large bird swooped down and deposited a fish at their feet.

Seizing it gratefully, the lad looked round for wood so that he could cook it for their dinner.

"Wait just one moment," said Cuthbert, holding out his hand. The boy gave him the fish and Cuthbert broke a piece off for the bird.

"God sent our dinner through him," he explained, "so he ought to have his share."

Birds and animals usually obeyed him: when he told them not to eat his little crop of barley, they dutifully gave the barley-field a miss. Offenders were sternly dealt with: some crows who persisted in feasting off the Lindisfarne monastery's thatched roof were solemnly banished. Three days later they returned, asking in crow-fashion for the saint's forgiveness and bringing, each in its own beak, a hunk of swine's lard as a peace-offering. Cuthbert pardoned the birds and graciously accepted the lard, which he kept for the use of visitors who made the wet journey to the island. And if you doubt *that* story, his monk-biographer would like you to know that he actually met people who had greased their boots with it!

Whether historical fact or pious legend, the host of Cuthbert-stories do give us a remarkably consistent picture of a kindly, cheerful, open-hearted man, no intellectual but full of common sense, a man who, despite his fasts and night-vigils, never seemed harsh or forbidding.

"He was always happy and joyful," says a contemporary. "He never wore a sad expression, if he remembered a sin which he had committed in the past, nor did he look pleased with himself if admirers praised his mode of life. His conversation was witty and down-to-earth. It consoled the sad, instructed the ignorant and appeased the angry; for he persuaded them all to let nothing come between them and the love of Christ."

As a Celtic monk Cuthbert lived his life in a cluster of small houses of stone or wattle, rather different in construction and layout from the solidly-built monasteries of later years. There were, of course, the familiar monastic buildings: chapel, refectory, store-houses and the rest. There was, however, no dormitory; each monk had a cell of his own, where he slept in his habit on a mattress and pillow.

The habit itself consisted of three main garments: a white tunic worn next to the skin, a combined cape and hood, and an apron or skirt which fastened round the waist. The monks wore shoes and an outer cloak during cold weather.

There were two meals each day: dinner at noon and supper during the evening, except Wednesdays and Fridays, which were fast days. Fish or eggs might be on the menu but never meat. During Lent, of course, the diet was severely curtailed.

Cuthbert's qualities soon brought him to the fore as Prior of Melrose under Boisil's successor, Eata. Both men were, inevitably, caught up in the Celtic-Roman con-

troversy. When they moved to Ripon, in Yorkshire, to set
up a new monastery, they were soon forced to hand it
over to the arch-Romaniser Wilfrid and to return to their
old base.

When the Synod of Whitby declared for Roman practice, Cuthbert and his Abbot loyally accepted the decision, hard though it must have been. At Lindisfarne, as
elsewhere, many of the community departed for Ireland
in protest. Cuthbert and Eata were now transferred to
the island monastery to bring the remainder into line
with the new regime.

Not surprisingly, they found a very unhappy atmo-
sphere. Of the monks who had stayed many were still
convinced that the Celtic way was the right way and
protested bitterly at the changes which were now forced
upon them. Cuthbert, however, refused to let the dispute
shatter the peace of the monastery. When voices were
raised in anger he simply brought the meeting to a close.
Next day he would go on with his talk as though nothing
had happened. Slowly but surely, under his influence,
peace descended over Lindisfarne once more.

Despite all his cheerfulness and his skill in handling
people, Cuthbert's closest relationship was with God. It
must have surprised the monks to see that their friendly,
down-to-earth Prior could never finish Mass without
shedding tears.

Cuthbert, for all his real love of people, began to feel a
growing desire for the solitary life of a hermit. At Lindisfarne there were often visitors, for the island could be
reached on foot at low tide. Just to the South, however,
lay some real islands, tiny and completely cut off by the
sea. On one of these, with the consent of Eata and his
brethren, Cuthbert built himself a home.

Alongside his little house and oratory lay a fresh-water

spring and a patch of barley which he planted for food.
Here, with birds and seals for company, Cuthbert had all
the solitude he wanted.

However, it was not to last. One day a boat from the
monastery arrived at his little landing-stage with the
news that Eata had been appointed Bishop of Hexham
and that Cuthbert was to be Bishop of Lindisfarne.

Cuthbert begged for six months more on his island. St.
Theodore, the Greek monk who was now Archbishop of
Canterbury, agreed. In the meantime the two candidates
exchanged Sees and it was as Bishop of Lindisfarne that
Cuthbert was ordained by Theodore in York Minster on
Easter Sunday, 685.

From now on his life resembled that of a modern missionary Bishop in some remote corner of the earth, without the motor transport, radio and other benefits which
are often available to even the poorest of today's missionaries. Northumbria *was* a remote corner of the earth
in those far-off times: a sparsely-populated kingdom
where a man could travel for miles over moorland and
mountain without seeing another human soul. Over this
wild terrain Cuthbert journeyed, winter and summer
alike, often on horseback, bringing the Gospel to those
who had not yet received it and encouraging Christians
who at any moment were all too likely to slide back into
the old pagan ways.

In the winter months a cruel North wind frequently
brought Arctic weather down from Scandinavia. During
one particularly savage winter, on a missionary trip to the
Picts of Galloway, Cuthbert and his companions wan-
dered for three days through deep snowdrifts, freezing
and without food, looking in vain for any sign of house or
village. His companions, convinced that death was inevitable, were ready to lie down and give up.

"Don't worry," Cuthbert assured them, "God will look after us."

Sure enough, by the rocks where the giant waves pounded, they found slices of dolphin's flesh. Hardly an appetising dish, you may think, but enough to sustain starving men until they reached shelter.

Many cures were attributed to him during these journeys—so many that it is impossible to believe that all the accounts are merely credulous tittle-tattle. He revived an apparently-dead boy with a kiss and a girl, dying in terrible pain, by anointing her with holy oil. When an earl's wife seemed about to breathe her last, Cuthbert told a priest to sprinkle her with holy water. She, too, recovered at once.

Like Christ at Cana he once turned water into wine— or at least he made it taste like wine, for apparently it did not change color. Whether or not it gained an added "kick," we are not told! Small wonder that, after miracles like these, Cuthbert became known as "the Wonder-Worker of Britain."

Unlike Aidan, a Gaelic speaker who never learned Anglo-Saxon, Cuthbert did not need an interpreter to go with him on his travels. A Northumbrian born, he spoke the local Anglo-Saxon dialect as a native.

During one of the terrible plague epidemics which swept the kingdom, Cuthbert worked so hard among the sick and dying that in the end he himself fell victim and was soon gravely ill. As he lay in bed, barely conscious, he heard the voices of his brethren chanting psalms and prayers for his recovery. To their astonishment, he suddenly sat up.

"What am I doing here in bed?" he demanded. "Surely God won't refuse to listen to men as holy as these!"

In no time he was back on the road, cheering his rav-
aged flock and tending their needs. But this time it was
no miracle; sheer will-power had forced Cuthbert back
to work. His health was seriously damaged and he never
recovered it.

As he felt death approaching, he returned once more to
his beloved hermitage on the island. As a hermit he had
never felt superior to his brother-monks; he always said
that a monk's life was superior to that of a solitary like
himself, because monks had to get along with each other
charitably and conform to discipline. When some of the
Lindisfarne community offered to come out and look
after him during these last days, he readily accepted; and
he asked especially that his nurses should include a
monk named Walstod who suffered from a severe bowel
complaint. Walstod was to be his last cure this side of the
grave.

Toward the end he lay in a corner of the little oratory
which he had built for himself, in pain but at peace. He
could not speak much, but when the brethren asked for a
farewell message to take back with them to Lindisfarne,
he urged them always to keep the peace among themselves and to be at peace also with all who worshipped
Christ.

"Don't despise others who keep the Faith and who
come to you for hospitality," he said. "Give them a big
welcome and entertain them kindly, then speed them on
their way. Don't think yourselves better than any other
Christian."

In these last hours the Celtic controversy was much on
his mind, for he twice warned his friends to have nothing
to do with schismatics who celebrated Easter at the
wrong time, or who otherwise harmed Catholic unity.
Cuthbert, whose early life had been so firmly rooted in
Celtic Christianity, now defended the Roman primacy

with his dying breath. He had seen the harm which the quarrel had done to the Church, and especially to his beloved Lindisfarne community, and he was determined that it should not break out again after his death.

"I know that during my life many people have despised me," he declared. "Yet when I am gone, you will see what sort of man I was and that my teaching did not deserve to be treated with contempt."

In the evening Cuthbert received Holy Communion, then lifted up his eyes and stretched out his arms. A little afterwards, as night fell, a monk carried two lighted torches to the water's edge. Across the dark waves, watchers on Lindisfarne saw the points of light moving slowly from side to side, and they knew that Cuthbert was dead.

3

The Quiet Man

One day in the year 680 or 681, a little boy of seven stood between his parents in the abbey of Monkwearmouth and presented bread, wine and money to the Abbot who smiled gravely down at him. Along with the gifts he handed over a paper, a petition asking that he be admitted to the monastery.

Of course young Bede did not become a monk at once, for he was much too young to take vows. Nevertheless, his monastic career effectively began at that moment. Along with the other lads in the monastery school he took part, day and night, in the chanting of the Divine Office: getting up at two or three in the morning for Prime and Terce, then going back to the dormitory for a few brief hours rest before lessons at six.

We can safely assume that Bede was the star pupil, always first with the answers and rarely, if ever, receiving the whacks which awaited the lazy or inattentive. From the first, he learned to love the Bible and the Office-prayers which took up much of the curriculum,

and soon he could read and write Latin as easily as he
could his native Anglo-Saxon.

From his teachers, too, he learned how Christianity
had come to Northumbria, and of the great Celtic-Roman
controversy that followed. Edwin and Paulinus, Aidan
and Hilda, Wilfrid and Oswy—soon he must have felt
as though he had known them all, so often were their
stories told and re-told. We can easily imagine the
eager-eyed youngster plying his teachers with question
after question, storing every detail in his capacious
memory.

Most of all his imagination was fired by Cuthbert,
whose legend was even then spreading rapidly throughout the kingdom. When Bede had first come to the monastery Cuthbert was still alive in his island hermitage. Now
he was dead but no less a friend to the sick and those in
trouble. A Bishop, gravely ill and in great pain, was
cured by a visit to Cuthbert's tomb. A young man whose
paralysis had defeated the doctors walked when he put
on Cuthbert's shoes. A hermit, his face terribly de-
formed, found himself whole after applying a piece of
calf's skin which had hung in Cuthbert's hermitage.

At this time, young Bede himself suffered from a hand-
icap, one which might well have prevented him, in future years, from handing on the knowledge which he was
so rapidly acquiring. We do not know the exact nature of
his speech impediment, nor do we know who suggested
that a relic of St. Cuthbert might bring the longed-for
cure. Cured he was, at all events, and he never afterwards forgot his gratitude to the saint whose biography
he would one day write.

While Bede was still in school, the Abbot of
Monkwearmouth, Benedict Biscop, opened a second
monastery at Jarrow, on the River Tyne, a few miles from

where the city of Newcastle now stands. Here Bede was
to spend the rest of his life.

Hardly had he settled into his new home when another
terrible plague, of the kind which had shortened
Cuthbert's life, broke out in the district. The Jarrow
monastery was, like every other, always vulnerable to disease: a germ-trap where people lived in close contact yet
knew little of elementary hygiene.

One by one the monks died, until there were only two
left who were sufficiently literate to keep up the daily
recitation of the Office. One was Ceolfrid, the sub-abbot
whom Benedict had put in charge at Jarrow; the other
was the boy Bede. Day after day they chanted on until
the plague subsided and new monks came to replace
those who had died. The experience must have made a
profound impression on the serious-minded youngster.
Did it, perhaps, make him wonder whether he had been
spared for some special purpose?

Though tucked away in a remote corner of the North-
east of England, the Jarrow monastery was no Celtic
backwater. By now the Church in Northumbria had been
absorbed into the mainstream of Roman Christianity.
Benedict Biscop actually visited Rome four times, making the last journey when he was well into his seventies.
Ceolfrid also made a pilgrimage there when he had
reached a similar ripe old age. Remembering the hazards
of eighth-century travel, we certainly have to admire the
courage of these holy old-timers!

Bede himself was to leave the monastery or its envi-
rons only three or four times in all his 55 years there, and
then he went no further than York and Lindisfarne.
(There is some evidence that Pope Agatho asked that he
be sent to Rome to advise on English affairs, but no evidence that he ever made the journey.) Yet the flow of

information between monasteries kept him in touch with
European learning, and in church he daily gazed upon
crosses and other ornaments which Benedict had
brought back from his travels in France and Italy.

Ordained a deacon at nineteen, Bede had to wait another eleven years before he was ordained priest, thirty
being the canonical age in those days. Both ceremonies
were performed by St. John of Beverley, who had been
one of Hilda's monks at Whitby.

By this time he was well established as a teacher in the
monastery school and we have a collection of notes
which he made for his students. Though its title, *On
Orthography,* makes it sound like a text-book on spelling, it really consists of random jottings which he put
down as they occurred to him or they arose in class. "One
should say 'drank half a glass' rather than 'drank half *the*
glass,'" writes Bede, "because one does not drink the
glass itself but what is in it."

These were busy, happy years in which Bede's writings, especially on Scripture, earned him fame far beyond Northumbria and beyond England itself. So famous
did he become that when a successor to Ceolfrid was
needed, Bede might have seemed the natural candidate.
In fact a monk named Hubert was chosen, perhaps because the brethren realised that teaching and writing
were Bede's real vocation and they did not want the
cares of office to distract him. Or it may just be that they
thought that Hubert would make a better Abbot.
Learned men are not necessarily able administrators—as
many a university has found to its cost!

At this time, too, Bede suffered a nasty shock, though it
would be nice to think that even he saw the funny side
later on. As he was busy about his books one day, a message from a friend named Plegwin, a monk in a neighbor-

ing monastery, informed him that some of the local
drunks were singing a song accusing him of heresy.

Naturally it was all a misunderstanding. In Bede's day
Scriptural exegesis dealt much in symbols and al-
legories. In particular it was usual to make the six-
water-pots of Cana symbolise the six ages of the world,
the sixth age being that of Our Lord's birth, circumcision,
presentation and subjection to His parents.

In a treatise on the subject Bede had given it as his
opinion that the fifth age ended and the sixth began with
the Incarnation. His inebriated critics read this as a de-
nial that Our Lord was born during the sixth age, this
being the traditional view. In fact they were wrong; Bede
had left that question open. Anyhow, as we now know,
no fundamental point of dogma was involved.

What we would all surely love to know is, who were
these theologically-minded topers? In the Eastern part of
the Roman Empire, it is true, ordinary layfolk argued
about the Trinity in shops and bath-houses, but we have
no evidence that it was so in Anglo-Saxon Northumbria.
There, we may feel fairly sure, tavern walls did not often
ring with doctrinal controversy.

Almost certainly, Bede's accusers were dissolute
monks whose easy interpretation of their Rule left room
for regular drinking bouts. Maybe they were members of
Pegwin's own monastery. As we shall see, in his last
years Bede worried much about the declining state of the
Church in his native kingdom and tried to exert his own
influence to improve matters.

The Scripture commentaries which won him so much
esteem among his contemporaries and throughout the
Middle Ages are today read by few apart from professional scholars. Their allegorical approach makes them
heavy going and although Bede did anticipate some

modern problems, much of his work has been overtaken
by latter-day research. Like all good scholars, he is self-
effacing; his books give us little insight into his personality. Yet an odd comment here and there shows how much
plain common-sense went along with all the learning.
Dealing with the disagreement between Paul and Bar-
nabas in the Acts of the Apostles, he observes: "It is not
wrong to be angry, but to be angry without strong and
just cause."

For us Bede's fame rests principally upon his great
Ecclesiastical History of the English Nation. Let no-one
be deterred by the title or by the fact that Bede originally
wrote it in Latin: this is one of the most fascinating and
thoroughly readable books ever produced by a major his-
torian. Though Bede went to enormous trouble to get his
facts right—he had friends check them for him in librar-
ies all over England and a London priest called Nothelm
went to Rome especially to do the necessary research
there—his *History* is no dry, pedestrian tome but a living
pageant in which episodes and personalities flash before
the eye with all the vividness of a fast-moving television
serial.

More important still, according to the present-day his-
torian E.S. Duckett, is the book's position as a national
epic, the *Aeneid* of England. Here, for the first time, the
English appear as one nation, the various tribes (Angles,
Saxons and Jutes) bound together by their common Faith
and by the organisation of the Church.

Beginning with the first converts during the Roman
occupation of Britain, Bede traces the path of English
Christianity over the 600 years to his own day. On the
way he tells stories which have been told and re-told
many times since he first set them down. Many of us
were only small when we first heard at school about Al-
ban, the Roman soldier who became a Christian and died

for his Faith; about old Coifi and the sparrow that pointed a kingdom toward Christianity; about the Synod of Whitby and the King who would not risk offending St. Peter.

The *History* was not Bede's own idea; he was asked to write it by Abbot Albinus of Canterbury. Although Albinus was not his Superior and lived at the opposite end of England, like a good monk, Bede obeyed. By the time he finished it, he was 58 and must have felt that his health was beginning to fail, for in his preface he asks his readers to pray for his many ills of mind and body.

The work was hard, certainly, and it took its toll. Yet Bede's enjoyment in his task shines out from every page. It was only now, when his career was almost at an end, that he could at last give range to his natural talent as a story-teller.

Did he realise that this might be his last work, and the one which would make his name live? Perhaps he did; for, before laying down his pen he set down, almost shyly, the main details of his life, as though driven by some inner compulsion to tell readers just a little about the man who toiled for so long over the book which he has left them.

After describing his arrival as a seven-year-old, he continues: "From that time on I have spent the whole of my life in the monastery. I devoted all my time to the study of Scripture; except, of course, when I was singing the Divine Office in church and carrying out all my other monastic duties. Learning, teaching and writing were always my delight. . . ."

It is indeed a delightful passage, a personal note from this most modest and retiring of saints.

Despite his life of prayer and scholarship, Bede had a deep pastoral concern for people outside the monastery walls. We know this from a letter which he wrote to

Egbert, the newly-ordained Bishop of York, on November 5, 734, barely six months before his own death.

Before his appointment, Egbert, too, had been a monk; he and Bede therefore speak the same language. Quite possibly Bede himself had, as a young priest, done some pastoral work. Since he lived at the point in history when the care of layfolk was passing from the monasteries to the newly-emerging dioceses, it is not too fanciful to imagine that, as he writes to Egbert, he is remembering his own days spent ministering in the villages around Jarrow. Now things have changed—and not for the better:

"Just as altar-vessels should not be put to improper use," Bede declares, "so it is altogether wicked and deplorable that a man ordained to say Mass and to speak and act in the Lord's name, should offend his Lord by empty and silly behaviour as soon as he leaves the church."

Worse is to come: even Bishops are now neglecting their duty. Partly this is because some of them, attracted by the prospect of a fat income, have taken on dioceses bigger than they can properly care for.

"It is common knowledge that many hamlets and farms in remote districts have not seen a Bishop for many years. Not only are these poor people deprived of Confirmation; there is nobody to instruct them in the Faith or to teach them the difference between right and wrong," he laments.

Bede's next comment is highly interesting because it shows him as a firm believer in the value of daily Communion for all—something that was not to become the norm again until the twentieth century:

"The daily reception of the Lord's Body and Blood is, as you know, the constant practice throughout Italy, France, Africa and the whole of the East. Here, however, this devotion and dedication to God is so much lacking—thanks to the carelessness of teachers—that in almost every part of the kingdom daily Communion is completely foreign to the laity. Even those who seem to be more devout do not venture to communicate except at Christmas, Epiphany and Easter."

As he looked from his cell-window across the gray Northumbrian fells, poor Bede found much else to depress him. Up and down the kingdom, noblemen were setting up their own "monasteries" and appointing themselves as Abbots in order to avoid military service. Some were even founding convents in which the Abbess was none other than the phoney Abbot's wife! There were other serious abuses besides these. Perhaps we can find a bleak sort of comfort in the thought that a community seemingly crammed with saints could have problems as bad as any in the Church of today.

It seems that Bede's letter bore fruit, for Egbert embarked on an energetic program of action. He had York upgraded to the status of an archdiocese (which it remains today, though belonging to the Anglican Church). This gave him supervisory powers over neighboring Bishops in the North of England and enabled to ensure that they did their jobs properly. He also founded the famous Cathedral School at York which, through its most famous pupil, Alcuin, was to become the forerunner of the great universities of Europe.

Bede was himself no mere bewailer of the time's evils; from his cell he worked to spread the Word. To help simple folk, he produced Anglo-Saxon versions of the Creed and the Lord's Prayer and he also translated Scripture and wrote other devotional works in the vernacular. He is, in fact, the first known writer of English prose, though unfortunately all these vernacular writings have now been lost.

Bede died on the Vigil of the Ascension, May 25, 735,

when the Church in her Divine Office had already begun
to celebrate the Feast. Thanks to a Jarrow monk named
Cuthbert, we have a complete and moving account of his
final hours.

During the early months of the year he had grown
steadily weaker and his brethren knew that he would not
be with them much longer. A fortnight before Easter, he
had serious difficulty in breathing and suffered a good
deal. From Easter to Rogationtide he rallied and was
serene and happy.

During all this time he went on studying and singing
the Office in choir, sleeping only for a short while at
night. He talked to his still-unlearned pupils in Anglo-
Saxon, turning his words more and more upon the soul's
journey from earth to the judgement-seat of God. At this
time he was translating into Anglo-Saxon both the Gospel of St. John and some passages from St. Isidore of
Seville.

On the Tuesday before Ascension Day, his breathing
once again became labored and his feet began to swell.
Yet still he worked on, dictating his translations to one or
other of the more literate young monks.

"Please hurry," he would urge when the pen seemed
to move too slowly, "I don't know how long I have to
live, or when my Creator will call me from here."

On Wednesday he began work as usual in the early
morning, to be interrupted briefly when the brethren left
for the Rogation procession, carrying saints' relics to beg
a blessing on the crops. As everyone knew how anxious
Bede was to finish his work, a boy named Wilbert was left
behind to act as secretary.

"There is one chapter left to translate," he told Bede,
"and it is hard for you to answer any more questions."

"No, it is easy," Bede replied. "Put you pen in the ink
and write quickly."

Though failing rapidly, Bede dictated on until the chapter was almost done. By now it was evening and his brother-monks had long returned from their procession. Feeling the end almost upon him, Bede asked Cuthbert to call all of them to his cell. One by one, he bade them farewell, giving to each a small present—pepper, a napkin or some incense—from the store that well-wishers had sent to him.

"The time of my going is almost here," he told them, "for my soul longs to gaze upon Christ, my King, in his beauty."

Some of the monks had been boys with him in the monastery school; others had been his pupils when he was still a young priest. Now that they were to lose their brother of so many years, they could scarcely speak in their sorrow. In the end it was young Wilbert's voice that broke the silence.

"Dearest Master," he said, "there is one more sentence yet to write."

"Good," replied Bede, "Let us write it."

He dictated the remaining words in a voice weak but audible. Wilbert wrote them, then laid down his pen.

"It is finished," he told the dying teacher.

"You have spoken the truth, my son," Bede replied. "It is finished."

Throughout this time Bede had been lying on the floor of the cell. Now he asked Wilbert to take his head in his hands and help him to lean against the wall, at the spot where he had for so many years said his prayers. His last prayer was the *Gloria,* which he chanted slowly and clearly. Then his life on earth ended.

For more than a thousand years Bede has been called "The Venerable" in special recognition of his holiness and learning. He is, significantly, the only Englishman whom Dante found in Paradise.

4

Scotland's Pearl

For many hours the crowd had been waiting. Now a murmur of excitement down-river told the watchers by the landing-stage that at last the royal ship was in sight. Lords and ladies, priests and merchants, cheeky cockney apprentices and gaping peasants from the countryside—all cheered lustily as the great vessel rounded the final bend in its journey up the Thames.

Ropes were thrown, she was made fast and the spectators craned forward eagerly for a first glimpse of the long-awaited passenger. Soon he was walking down the gangway, his family behind him; and behind them a brightly-dressed entourage of nobles and courtiers who chattered to each other in a strange, barbaric-sounding tongue.

On the landing-stage stood the King, Edward the Confessor, a kindly, grave-faced man who now stepped forward to greet this other Edward whom he had summoned from exile to become his heir apparent. Though Edward Aetheling was now forty-one, this was his first good look at the England which he had been invited to rule, once the Confessor was dead.

He and his twin brother, Edmund, had been only a few
months old when their father, Edmund Ironside, fell
under the Viking swords, leaving Danish King Canute as
undisputed ruler of England. Canute, never a man to
take chances, decided to have the two infants quietly
killed. Not daring to murder them on English soil, he
despatched them to his cousin, King Olaf of Sweden,
with a strong hint that they could be done away with
there. Olaf, himself a good Christian, sent the little Saxon
princes to Stephen, the saintly King of Hungary.

Of young Edmund no more is heard: presumably he
died in childhood. Edward, however, grew up in Hungary and married a Bavarian princess who gave him a son
named Edgar and two daughters, Margaret and Christina. They, of course, accompanied their father now that,
with England once more in Saxon hands, he had been
summoned home to become heir-apparent to the throne.

Within moments of setting foot on English soil, the two
princesses stole the scene. The Londoners, who had
turned out to greet their future king, nudged each other
excitedly as they caught their first glimpse of his
daughters, beautiful girls with auburn hair, blue eyes
and unmistakably Saxon features. For Margaret, especially, there were gasps of admiration. Though still only
a child, she moved with a grace and composure which, in
any surroundings, would immediately have marked her
out as royal. At twelve years of age, young Margaret
looked every inch a queen.

Her father never did become King of England. Within
a few short months of his arrival in England he was
dead—from what cause we do not know. Some historians
think he may have been murdered, though by whom and
from what motive none can say.

In Hungary the family had been under the protection
of Stephen, who was both a king and a saint. Now, in

England, the orphaned youngsters had another saint-
king to look after them. The times, indeed, were troubled; powerful Saxon barons challenged the Confessor's
rule and the Norman Duke William was already casting
envious eyes across the English Channel. Nevertheless
their growing years were happy as they absorbed the
customs and the language, not only of England but of
Normandy too; for the Confessor's mother had been a
Norman princess and he himself had grown up in exile
there.

The girls, studious and devout, both prepared to enter
the religious life. Edgar, the only son, might in more
normal times have become heir-apparent in his father's
place. But poor Edgar, though a pleasant enough lad and
no fool, was not of the stuff from which kings are made.
Shortly before he died, on January 5, 1066, Edward the
Confessor named a native-born Saxon prince, Harold, as
his successor.

Nine months later, as all the world remembers, the
Normans invaded and came face to face with Harold's
forces on a field near the Sussex village of Hastings.
Harold fell dead, his eye and brain pierced by a Norman
arrow, and William the Conqueror became King of England.

It was young Edgar, the man who might have been
King, who actually handed the crown of England to William. The coronation ceremony took place on Christmas
Day, 1066, in the great abbey which Edward had built at
Westminster—and where English monarchs are crowned
to this day. Despite this act of fealty, the Aetheling family did not feel safe. King Canute had seen their father's
very existence as a threat, even though he was then only
a tiny baby. Might not Edgar, timid and inoffensive
though he was, arouse similar feelings in the Conqueror?

Two years later, in 1068, Saxons in the North of England revolted. William, interrupted in a hunting trip, marched North and put down the rebellion with his usual ruthless efficiency. The Aethelings judged that the time had come to fly.

Slipping up the East coast by boat, the royal refugees eventually put into the mouth of the River Wear, close to the spot where Bede had begun his monastic career. There they threw themselves on the mercy of Malcolm, the fierce Scots King who, by defeating Macbeth, had both won his throne and avenged his father's death. For fifteen years before that, he himself had lived in exile at the English court, leaving in the year that Margaret and her family arrived. It is possible, therefore, that they and Malcolm already knew each other.

Malcolm was a man of strong passions, capable of great affection and equal cruelty. At that moment he was waging a punitive campaign against the English Earl of Northumberland, who had made the mistake of invading what was then Scottish territory. Totally without mercy, Malcolm's troops slaughtered old men and women, tossed babies on swords and drove the able-bodied young of both sexes back to Scotland as slaves. Those who collapsed on the journey were either killed or left to die.

Breaking off from this bloodthirsty work, Malcolm received the fugitives kindly and promised shelter for themselves and their retinue. These included several Hungarian nobles who had travelled with them from their earlier exile. They, too, settled in Scotland and were ultimately absorbed into its national life. It is said that the well-known Leslie family was originally Leleszi.

Many a happy union is based on the attraction of opposites, so we need not be too surprised that very soon the fierce warrior-king was head over heels in love with the cultured and devout Margaret. Though his affection was real enough, Malcolm no doubt had an eye to the political advantage which marriage to an English princess would bring.

After much prayer and counsel, Margaret was convinced that her vocation lay, not in the cloister, but as Queen, wife and mother. At the time of her marriage she was about twenty-two years old. Her husband, a widower nearing forty, already had a son by his first wife.

To this learned, cosmopolitan young woman, brought up in the mainstream of European culture, the country which she now adopted must have seemed strange and barbarous indeed. Its nobles, rude and warlike, spoke a language unlike any which she had ever heard. Its Church, though formally in communion with Rome, had, like the Celtic Church of old, developed practices which differed considerably from those generally considered orthodox.

From the beginning Margaret saw her life-work clearly. She understood why God had led her to Scotland and the throne. She must bring civilisation, Saxon and Norman, to these wild Gaels, and she must bring their wayward Church into line with Rome.

Before she could do any of this, she must fire her husband with at least some of her own ideals. According to her biographer, a monk named Turgot, she soon succeeded; indeed Turgot would have us believe that she turned her wild Malcolm into something of a gentleman. "Influenced by her zeal and industry," he wrote dutifully, "the King laid aside his barbarity of manners and became more honorable and refined."

Just how honorable and refined Malcolm became is a matter of conjecture. We know that on several occasions he swore fealty to the Norman King across the border, only to break his oath at the earliest opportunity in order to go rampaging into English territory. Malcolm gave up fighting the way some people give up smoking and, as we shall see, the habit was to be the death of him.

Though she effected no miraculous transformation, Margaret nevertheless did bring out the best in her ferocious husband. She achieved this, I need hardly say, by example rather than by exhortation. Her prayers, her constant fasts, above all her deep love for the poor, all made a profound impact on the King.

Margaret really did love the poor; she was no mere Lady Bountiful sallying forth to distribute handouts before bolting back to the luxury of the palace. Every day in Lent, for example, she served dinner to three hundred poor people with her own hands. Soon Malcolm, no doubt self-consciously at first, joined her in handing round the dishes. She wanted him to help and he surrendered without a fight. He could refuse her nothing. When she raided his cash-box, as she often did, for money to give to some destitute subject, he uttered no word of protest. On one occasion he actually caught her in the act and laughingly threatened to have her tried and condemned for theft.

The plight of the English captives, now working as slaves up and down Scotland, naturally roused her special pity. By sending out her own spies she discovered which were being worst treated, paid their ransom and had them sent home. Where this was not possible, she saw to it that conditions were improved.

Nobody could blame Malcolm for doting on his lovely young queen. All the same, it might have been better if he had put his foot down now and again, especially in the matter of her fasting. Like more than one other saint, Margaret overdid this so drastically that in the end she damaged her health permanently and was in constant pain, probably from an ulcer.

Margaret bore Malcolm eight children and, even though she herself had grown up in exile and was now Queen of Scotland, she gave each of them an English name. (Her own name comes, of course, from the Greek word for "pearl.")

Sadly, none of the eight left behind any account of their childhood, nor do we have any comment which would tell us how they felt toward their mother. We know that the royal steward had orders to whip them if they were naughty, but in this Margaret was no more strict than other parents of the Middle Ages, many of whom—among the upper classes at least—subjected their children to punishments of barbaric harshness, often carried out by other people. The two girls, Matilda and Mary, were sent for their education to Aunt Christina, now Abbess of a convent at Romsey in Southern England. There, it is reported, they went in fear of her sharp tongue and her even sharper rod.

Margaret's personality was certainly gentler, yet she must have been an awe-inspiring parent all the same. For of what other mother was it said that she never laughed and never lost her temper?

She loved to teach the little ones, whom she called— we are relieved to hear—her "darlings." We can imagine them gathered about her, round-eyed and solemn, as she gravely warned them to fear the Lord always, and so get good fortune in this life and eternal happiness in the next. She wrote out a rule of life for them, of which the first injunction, quoted many times down the centuries, was that they should be prepared to die a thousand deaths rather than commit a single mortal sin.

They were told, too, always to take special care of orphans, and here Margaret set the example by having orphan babies brought regularly to the palace. The Queen herself fed them, preparing the baby-food with her own

hands, then sitting them on her knee while they dined
from the royal spoons. During her travels round Scotland
she was always accompanied by twenty-four poor people
who lived at her expense and were served their meals
before Margaret got hers.

Though state banquets were part of her job, Margaret
had little taste for them. Even when she was not actually
fasting, she ate very sparingly. Nobles who overloaded
their tables—and their stomachs—felt distinctly uncomfortable as they watched the Queen chatting quite happily over a portion that would scarcely feed a sparrow.

Despite their mutual devotion, Margaret and Malcolm
had at least one bad moment in their marriage. It happened because Margaret, whenever court routine gave
her a chance, liked to slip away to a secret spot in the
woods where she could pray alone. Malcolm, always
jealous and suspicious by nature, decided that she must
be meeting a lover and resolved to catch the two of them
in their hiding-place. When he got there, however, he
found no lover but only his wife, on her knees and praying in a low voice for him. Her devotions over, she rose
and began the journey home, only to discover her husband, prostrate on the ground and weeping with remorse.

With her enormous capacity for self-denial, it might
easily be imagined that Margaret was somber in her
dress. After all, she had originally wanted to be a nun.
Yet though her monk-biographer—a friend of the
family—insists that she hated outward show, the fact is
that she wore splendid clothes. She ran an embroidery-
school for the court ladies, where neither husbands nor
boy-friends were allowed to interrupt the stitching, and
she invited merchants from England and from other
European countries to bring rich textiles to Scotland.

Soon Malcolm's rather scruffy courtiers were decking
themselves in unaccustomed finery.

No doubt Margaret considered it a Queen's duty to
encourage the court to smarten itself up, but I cannot
help wondering whether she did not actually enjoy the
process just a little. For the Queen, despite all her asceticism, had superb taste in most things, and her influence
can be seen to this day.

Not only were textile merchants invited to Scotland;
builders and stone-masons were called in to erect new
churches and monasteries, and to refurbish existing ones.
Soon the bare Celtic style had been cross-fertilised by
the new richness of decoration from Europe.

In Dunfermline, the city where the royal couple had
been married, she laid the foundations of the great abbey
where both of them now lie buried. When one of her sons
succeeded to the throne as David 1, he carried on the
work which his mother had begun. To David, Scotland
owes many of its finest medieval buildings.

If Margaret influenced church building, she made a
bigger impact on the living Church of the time. In their
drift from Roman ways, the Scots had reverted to the
primitive practice of beginning Lent on the Monday following Ash Wednesday instead of on Ash Wednesday
itself. Stepsons were permitted to marry step-mothers
and a brother-in-law could marry his deceased brother's
wife. Even more quaintly, some Scots kept Saturday holy
instead of Sunday, like modern Seventh-day Adventists.
There were also complaints about "barbarous rites"—
which may simply have meant that the Scots, somewhat
ahead of their time, celebrated Mass in Gaelic!

The most distressing lapse—and it certainly distressed
Margaret—was the misplaced reverence which made
them reluctant to go to Holy Communion even at Easter.

This was based on a too-scrupulous reading of St. Paul's warning that those who receive unworthily eat and drink judgement to themselves.

"If they are right in staying away from the Sacrament," demanded Margaret, "Why did Jesus say that unless we eat the flesh of the Son of Man and drink His blood we shall not have life?"

Nobody who had heard her debate theology with learned priests would have doubted her ability in that direction, and when she proposed that a Council should be called to rid the local Church of its errors, Malcolm made no demur. Indeed, when the time came he actually lent his services an interpreter to the English clerics who were called in to enlighten their Scots brethren. The "Council of the Five Points" succeeded in its aim, though curiously it made no mention of one of the most serious abuses of the time: the holding of monasteries and monastic lands in lay hands.

Every day, in one way or another, Margaret influenced her adopted country for the better. If you ever take a boat across the Firth of Forth, don't forget to say a prayer to her, for she set up a ferry-service there long ago and to this day the towns at either end are called North and South Queensferry. Another memento is a boulder, known as St. Margaret's Stone, on the North Queensferry Road just outside Dundermline. Here, it is said, Margaret used to sit when she settled legal disputes for the poor—a judicial function which Malcolm was no doubt glad to leave to his clever wife.

Margaret and Malcolm were the first royal couple to spend part of their time at Edinburgh, now Scotland's capital, where the great rock with its castle still looms over the city. Here, in the little oratory which still stands, the gravely-ill Queen heard Mass for the last time on a November day in 1093. Her husband was far away in

Northumbria, fighting yet another battle. Not even her entreaties had been sufficient to prevent him. Now they brought her news that he was dead, struck down by a traitor's hand. Four days later she followed him, a royal lady whom Scotland has never forgotten and, incidentally, an ancestor of Britain's present Queen.

5

Murder at Canterbury

The day was bitterly cold and the beggar's teeth chattered audibly as King Henry the Second and his Chancellor, Thomas Becket, rode over the ice-covered cobbles, with the courtiers clattering along at a respectful distance behind.

Any out-of-town stranger in the London crowd, trying to guess which was Henry and which the Chancellor, would probably have guessed wrong. Henry, who cared nothing for his appearance, had wrapped himself in a drab, mud-spattered cloak. Thomas, a cleric in deacon's orders, sported an elegant new cape of gray and scarlet. Whatever Thomas wore, it was invariably new.

As they rode through the capital this winter morning, laughing together at some shared joke, Henry suddenly caught sight of the beggar, pressed back with the rest of the crowd against the wooden buildings. Often he had twitted his friend for wearing a fortune on his back. Now he intended to have some fun with him.

"Thomas, do you see that poor fellow shivering in those miserable rags?" he demanded.

59

"Why yes, your majesty," replied Thomas with a puzzled lift of the eyebrow.

"Don't you think, now, that it would be a fitting act of Christian charity to provide him with a nice warm cloak to keep out the winter chill?" The King's expression gave no hint of any joke.

"Indeed it would, Sir," said Thomas. "I suggest you see to the matter right away."

"No, Thomas," the King responded gravely, "you are going to do that! "

With a sudden lunge and a roar of laughter, he grabbed at Thomas's cape. Thomas, still agile at 36, ducked swiftly out of the way. The scuffle that followed, punctuated by shouts of mirth, several times seemed as though it would drag both King and Chancellor from their horses and land them sprawling on the cobblestones. On both sides of the street the spectators stood popeyed with astonishment. The courtiers, used to such scenes, only smiled.

Within minutes the cape had been surrendered. The beggar, scarcely able to believe his luck, wrapped it round him and stammered his thanks to the still-laughing monarch. With a rueful grin Thomas accepted a courtier's cloak in its place and the royal procession clattered on its way.

Thomas did not spend much time mourning the lost garment, for he had a splendid wardrobe at home and in any case a medieval Chancellor had many more important things to occupy his mind. State treasurer, commander-in-chief of the army, foreign minister, judge, minister of public works, dispenser of royal charters . . . all these duties were combined in his own person. He accompanied the monarch when he went on tour and advised him in all governmental matters.

Apart from his official functions, Thomas was also the

King's best friend. He went with Henry on his frequent hunting and fowling expeditions, for these were sports which Thomas himself loved and at which he excelled.

Once, as a boy, he had fallen into a mill-race while attempting to rescue a hawk which had crash-dived into the water. As the current dragged him towards the great flailing wheel, the miller, knowing nothing of his plight, decided to bring it to a standstill. Only then did he discover that he had saved Thomas from certain death. . . .

Thomas Becket was born on the feast of St. Thomas the Apostle, December 21. The year was probably 1118; the place, we know for certain, was his father's house in Cheapside, the London street which still winds through the ancient square mile called the City. Since surnames were only then coming into general use, young Becket was known during his earlier life as Thomas of London.

Both his parents were Norman immigrants. His father, a successful merchant, had served as a Sheriff of the City. Of his mother we know little save that she was gracious, kind and devout. Legend says that she used to weigh out gifts for the poor by putting the food and money in one side of the scale and her baby boy in the other.

Though he had a quick brain and an absorbent memory, Thomas was not notably studious: that came later. Meanwhile, hawks and horses were more attractive than books, though he did also excel at chess and his love of the game remained with him throughout his life.

For his later studies Thomas was sent to Paris, where he may have attended the lectures of the great theologian, Peter Abelard. His schooling over, he went into the office of a relative who was one of the Sheriffs responsible for governing the city—an office which, as we have seen, Thomas's father had held earlier. Now Thomas was himself part of the same administration, treading the corridors of power for the first time.

He must have enjoyed the work, yet he did not stay.
After only three years at his City desk, Thomas Becket
turned his eyes toward Canterbury.

For an ambitious young man the Church was an obvious stepping-stone to power and wealth, and nobody
really knows today whether Thomas's sights were set on
these worldly targets, or whether he felt the first stirrings
of his future vocation to the priesthood. Perhaps he always intended to be ordained, for there is a tradition that
his parents had dedicated him to the Church when he
was still an infant. The death of his dearly-loved mother,
when he was twenty-one, had affected him deeply and
this, too, may have played a part in his decision.

Whatever his motives may have been, in the winter of
1143–4 Thomas entered the service of Theobald, Archbishop of Canterbury. Among the brilliant young men
who surrounded England's senior prelate, Thomas of
London immediately stood out. When the others realised
that the newcomer was a favorite whom Theobald intended to promote, the inevitable jealousy made itself
felt. Like executives jockeying for position in a modern
corporation, some of the more ambitious clerics were not
above stabbing a rival in the back. Thomas's particular
enemy, one Roger of Pont L'Eveque, twice succeeded in
having him fired on trumped-up charges. Each time,
however, Thomas was subsequently cleared and rein-
stated.

Tall, slimly-built and pale, with dark hair and a long
nose, Thomas Becket was, according to a friend, "blithe
of countenance, winning and loveable in his conversation, but slightly stuttering in his talk." The stutter does
not seem to have done his career any harm, either now or
later. He had the gift, invaluable to an administrator, of
grasping a complex problem quickly and expressing it in
a straightforward manner. Recognising this talent,

Theobald sent him to Bologna for a year's study of civil and canon law.

When the Archbishop, in defiance of King Stephen's wishes, slipped out of England on a visit to Pope Eugenius 111, it was Thomas whom he chose as his companion. They crossed the English Channel by night in a leaky old tub that nearly sank. "Sounds as though you swam here rather than sailed," said the Pope.

In 1154 Thomas was appointed Archdeacon of Canterbury, at which point he received his deacon's orders. This appointment made him officially Theobald's right-hand man: the elderly Archbishop did nothing without consulting him and sent him on several more missions to Rome. Not only was Thomas now powerful, he was also rich, the holder of sinecures in cathedrals and parishes which he hardly ever visited, but which nevertheless provided him with a fat income.

In December of that same year, Henry, Duke of Normandy, was crowned King of England. Archbishop Theobald, probably with his new archdeacon's aid, had conducted the negotiations which brought him to the throne. When the young King Henry the Second looked around for a Chancellor, Theobald pointed to Thomas Becket.

Though still only twenty-one, Henry had won his crown by invading England, bringing half the nation under his control and withdrawing only on a promise that he would be named as Stephen's heir. He was destined to become one of the greatest of all English kings, a superb administrator whose reform of the legal system, in particular, brought benefits which have lasted to the present day.

Yet in his personal life Henry was totally disorganised, endlessly changing his plans and driving his household crazy in the process. If the King announced that he would set off early for a particular place, one courtier complained bitterly, you could safely assume that he would sleep until noon, and vice versa. A stocky, red-haired man with a fierce expression and a cracked voice, he was nevertheless capable of great affection, and of inspiring it in others.

In naming Thomas his Chancellor it seemed that he had made a perfect choice: an organiser and diplomat whose talents matched his own. Though Thomas was fifteen years older he had a boyish heart which responded eagerly to the King's rumbustious humor.

Thomas's love of magnificence amazed everyone. When he went on a diplomatic mission to Louis VII of France, his retinue included two hundred knights and other gentlemen, all on horseback, and hundreds more servants, soldiers and footboys who sang as they marched. For his own wardrobe he took twenty-four suits which he wore once and then gave away, and among the presents for his hosts were loads of silk cloaks, furs, hangings, carpets, hawks, hounds, monkeys and mastiffs. Eighty-five carts carried this and other luggage; two of them were loaded with a specially-brewed beer in metal casks, dark and wine-colored to suit Gallic taste.

"If this is the Chancellor's turn-out," asked the gaping Frenchmen, "what must the King's be like?"

Rich, ambitious, revelling in pomp and luxury—they are hardly the qualities which we look for in a future saint. Yet even when his worldly career was at its height, Thomas's more observant guests noticed that he ate sparingly of the food at his groaning table. Some may even have heard it whispered that this magnificent Chancellor spent hours at night in prayer and that he often rose at dawn to pray at some church-door. Though he gave presents openly to great men, as his position demanded, he also gave generously and in secret to the poor.

From time to time his friends knew, he went on retreat to the monks of Merton, whose school he had attended as a boy. For a cleric in his position temptations were many, yet his life was always chaste.

In 1159 Henry went to war in France to recover his wife's province of Toulouse. Leading several hundred of his own knights into battle, Thomas showed himself a brave and able general, carrying out assaults in full armor and engaging in hand-to-hand encounters with the enemy.

Meeting him in his battle-gear, the Prior of Leicester was shocked. "Aren't you supposed to be a cleric?" he demanded. "You hold I don't know how many important benefices—and from what I hear, you are to be the next Archbishop of Canterbury!"

"Then I hope you hear wrongly," retorted Thomas. "I know three poor priests in England whom I would far rather see made Archbishop than myself. If I were promoted, I should either have to lose the King's favor or neglect my duty to God."

Thomas's reluctance was sincere, for he well knew the conflicts which he would face if he became leader of the Church in England. Like his tough Norman predecessors Henry was quite ready to infringe on the Church's rights in order to keep power in his own hands. Several times already, Thomas's conscience had been torn and we know that some of his decisions as Chancellor had deeply disappointed his old master, Theobald.

When Henry tried to force a high-born abbess into a political marriage, however, Thomas showed his mettle. As Chancellor he was also the royal chaplain, the "keeper of the King's conscience," and he told Henry firmly that he could not lawfully compel a nun to give up her vows. He made sure, furthermore, that no dispensation was forthcoming from Rome.

The affair might have shown Henry what to expect if
Thomas became Archbishop. Nevertheless, when
Theobald died in 1161, Henry told Thomas that he
wanted him to succeed to the See of Canterbury. Thomas
now warned the King directly that his promotion would
mean the end of their friendship. "The affection with
which you honor me would be changed to hatred," he
declared.

His protests were overruled both by Henry and by
Rome. On Saturday, June 3, 1162, Thomas was ordained
priest. The next day, the Octave of Pentecost, he was
consecrated Archbishop.

"Watch my behavior carefully and warn me of my
faults, for four eyes see better than two." Thomas's request, made to his clergy on the road to Canterbury,
shows his determination to lead a new and better life.
Popular legend credits him with an overnight conversion
from playboy to saint, and he himself said that he
changed from being "a patron of play-actors and a fol-
lower of hounds to being a shepherd of souls." As we
have seen, his conversion was neither so sudden nor so
simple as is often supposed.

That there *was* a conversion, and a dramatic one, nobody can deny. Next to his skin this once-fastidious
dandy wore a hair-shirt which, since he never changed it,
was soon alive with vermin.

As Archbishop he was also head of Canterbury's
monastic community and his life was now governed by
monastic hours. With the monks he rose at midnight to
sing the Office, then he washed the feet of thirteen poor
men and gave them money. At dawn he went to bed but
was up again for Mass at nine, though out of reverence he
did not always celebrate it himself. When he was the
celebrant, tears filled his eyes as he put on the vestments.

He gave out more alms afterwards, took a siesta in the

early afternoon and dined with colleagues and guests at three. Keeping a generous table for the sake of others, he ate more frugally than ever—though, no doubt to put others at ease, he drank a little wine and tasted one of the more attractive dishes.

On one occasion a visiting monk noticed this and smiled. Thomas guessed what was passing through his mind.

"If I am not mistaken, Brother," he observed gently, "there is more greediness in your eating beans than in my eating pheasant." This was true, for "quantity, not quality" was the monk's motto and he liked to stuff himself with approved monastic fare.

On his appointment as Archbishop, Thomas had resigned his post as Chancellor, Henry, though not pleased, continued to treat him as a friend.

The first rift came when Thomas refused to pay to the Crown a land-tax which had previously been voluntary.

"By God's eyes, this shall be paid!" the King swore.

"By the reverence of those eyes, my lord King" replied Thomas, "not a penny shall be paid from my lands."

Henry did not force the issue, but his resentment smoldered. It was only a matter of time before some new and worse quarrel would damage relations seriously.

The man who sparked it off was a canon named Philip de Brois. Tried for murder and acquitted in the Bishop of Lincoln's court, he was summoned to appear in the King's court. This summons he refused in offensive terms and was further charged with contempt.

Thomas asked that his court be allowed to try Philip for both offences. Henry reluctantly agreed. Though the Archbishop's court found Philip guilty of the contempt, Henry thought the resulting sentence too light. More conflicts of the same kind followed. In October, 1163, the

King formally demanded that all clergy convicted of
criminal offences be handed over to the civil power for
punishment.

In fairness to Henry, it should be pointed out that the
term "clergy" included not only priests and deacons, but
anyone who could claim to be in minor orders, in effect,
anyone who worked for the Church and could read and
write a little Latin. On the other hand, to deliver to the
King's court someone who had already been dealt with
by an ecclesiastical court was to risk punishing him
twice.

Some of the Bishops were inclined to give in to Henry,
but they let Thomas do the talking. Predictably he told
Henry in plain terms that only the Church could judge
and punish a criminal cleric; from the beginning this had
been canon law throughout Christendom and nothing
could change it.

Poor Henry! His pain and confusion must have been
very real. A strong King, surrounded by yes-men, he was
not used to opposition from any of his subjects. Yet here
was his old friend Thomas, the man whom he had trusted
above all, openly defying him in front of a whole roomful
of Bishops.

In something like desperation, he demanded that the
Church respect his royal "customs," though what these
might be he did not specify. Thomas and his colleagues
agreed, "saving our consecration and the unimpaired
rights of God." This carefully-hedged response provoked
Henry to further rage and the meeting broke up in disor-
der.

At the Council of Clarendon, held in the following
year, the King laid his "customs" on the table. Among
other things he demanded wide rights over excommuni-
cations, vacant Church appointments, appeals to Rome
and the movement of clerics out of the country. Signifi-

cantly, he repeated his earlier demand that clerics convicted by Church courts should be handed over to the
royal judges.

Pope Alexander 111, who had problems of his own,
was at first inclined to be conciliatory. Taking his cue
from the Pope, Thomas weakened briefly and promised
to accept Henry's demands. When Alexander saw the
King's list, however, he reacted angrily.

"By the Lord Almighty," he declared, "no seal of mine
shall be put to them!"

Thomas, ashamed of his earlier weakness, went back
on his word, while at the same time trying to heal the
breach with the King. His effort was futile: Henry would
not even see his old friend.

With the obvious intention of ruining Thomas, Henry
now sued him for a large sum of money said to be owing
from his time as Chancellor, though in fact the debt had
been discharged. He was further charged with contempt
for failing to appear in the King's court when summoned,
and he was ordered to produce Chancery accounts.

The "trial" which followed at Northampton Castle was
a bizarre proceeding, Thomas remaining on the ground
floor while his accusers and judges did their worst upstairs. We know neither the charge nor the sentence,
though the shouts of "Traitor!" which ended the session
may provide a clue.

Immediately afterwards, some of the barons stormed
downstairs and picked up rushes and rubbish from the
floor to hurl at the Archbishop. Called a traitor to his face,
Thomas showed a flash of his old fire.

"You lout!" he stormed at one of his chief tormentors.
"If I were not a priest, this right hand would prove what
a liar you are!"

That night, disguised as a humble lay-brother, Thomas
fled to France, taking shelter in friendly monasteries

until he reached the coast. "Brother Christian" had trouble in hiding his identity: soon after he crossed the Channel an innkeeper's wife recognised him and another time he nearly gave himself away by casting a too-appraising eye at a hawk perched on a knight's wrist.

His exile lasted for six years. During the whole of this time he lived as a humble monk, first with the Cistercians of Pontigny and then with the Benedictines of Sens.

Meanwhile negotiations for a settlement went on, not eased by Thomas's hard-line attitude. In 1170 came a crisis. Henry's young son, Henry junior, was crowned as heir-apparent by Thomas's old enemy, Roger of Pont L'Eveque, now Archbishop of York. Only the Archbishop of Canterbury had the right to perform this ceremony, which had gone ahead in defiance of a last-minute prohibition from the Pope.

The threat of a papal interdict—which would have barred the whole nation from the Sacraments—brought about the long-awaited reconciliation. When Henry and Thomas met in Normandy, the King had tears in his eyes as he pleaded that bygones should be bygones. So much affection did he show for his old friend that it seemed for a moment as though nothing had ever been wrong.

The reconciliation was phoney, as Thomas well knew. The disputed coronation was still an issue between them and other outstanding problems were not even mentioned.

"My Lord," said Thomas before he left for England, "my heart tells me that I depart as one whom you will not see again."

"Do you count me faithless then, Thomas?" asked the King.

"May you never be so, my Lord," replied the Archbishop.

His fellow-countrymen gave him a tumultuous welcome: when his ship was sighted, humble people rushed into the sea to get his blessing. Henry, meanwhile, was once more in a towering rage, for he had just learned that Thomas had suspended Roger and the other bishops who had helped to crown his son.

"While Becket lives, you will have no good days, nor quiet times, nor a tranquil kingdom." Almost certainly it was Roger who poured the poison into Henry's ear, for he had gone to France with two of his fellow-Bishops to complain of Thomas's latest piece of high-handedness. The words, whoever spoke them, provoked Henry's fateful outburst:

"What disloyal cowards do I have in my court that none will rid me of this low-born priest!"

Most of us have at some time uttered words that we would later give anything to unsay. Henry, a man of sudden and violent passions, almost certainly did not deliberately intend Thomas's murder. Yet four of his knights chose to take him at his word and, as though they feared that he might stop them, at once left secretly for England.

Reginald FitzUrse, William de Tracy, Hugh de Morville, Richard le Breton . . . but for the crime which they committed, who would now remember their names? They arrived at Canterbury on the afternoon of Tuesday, December 29, 1170. Marching into the Archbishop's palace, they confronted Thomas and demanded that he lift the suspensions on Roger and his colleagues. Thomas, who had been warned of their coming, refused.

Bawling threats and curses, they stamped off to put on their armor and to rally their men, no doubt aware that Thomas could call on knights of his own to defend him. As twilight fell, they returned, breaking down doors as they battered their way through the palace in search of their victim.

Thomas awaited them calmly in his bedroom, where he had told them that they would find him. His terrified attendants had other plans; they tried to drag him bodily to the cathedral, where they imagined that the law of sanctuary would keep him safe.

Thomas resisted at first, but in the end agreed to walk to the cathedral in a dignified manner, with his cross carried before him. The procession began but Thomas walked too slowly for the attendants, who tried desperately to hustle him along.

When eventually they arrived inside the cathedral, Vespers were being sung. Thomas found himself facing a crowd of monks whose fear had made them forget what they were about.

"Get back into choir," Thomas commanded. "I won't come in while you are standing there."

Half-obeying him, the monks moved back. Behind them in the gloom, armed men could be seen. Some of the monks, in their panic, slammed the door and bolted it, shutting out several of their brethren who now beat loudly on the other side. Thomas, hearing the racket, turned back.

"This is a church, not a fortress," he thundered. "Open the door and let anyone enter who wishes!"

As the knights in their armor strode towards him, three men stayed at his side. Soon two of those had retreated and only a monk named Edward Grim remained. Once more the knights demanded that Thomas absolve the Bishops and once more he refused.

It was Tracy who struck the first blow. Edward Grim warded it off with his arm but it grazed Thomas's head and blood ran down into his eyes.

"Into thy hands, O Lord, I commend my spirit," murmured Thomas, who had covered his face. And, as another blow fell: "For the name of Jesus and for His Church, I am ready to die."

He pitched forward on to his face. With a blow whose force broke his sword against the pavement, Le Breton clove his skull. Hugh of Horsea, a sub-deacon who had joined the murderers, scattered Thomas's brains over the pavement with his sword-point.

When news of his death was brought to Henry, he shut himself up lamenting and fasted for forty days.

6

The Lion and the Swan

To the bully-boys of Lincoln it seemed like a good idea at the time. Their betters were away in the Holy Land, fighting the infidel. What better way to show their support than by killing off the local Jews?

However, this was one pogrom that never got off the ground. In Lincoln's great cathedral, which today still rides high over the city, a stockily-built Frenchman from Burgundy faced the armed mob and told them, in words which stung each man to his soul, exactly how the Lord would reward those who sought to honor him by murdering his kinsfolk. As the would-be persecutors shuffled out of the cathedral, all thoughts of murder, synagogue-burning and loot had been banished from their minds. Instead there was only the memory of those stinging words, those flashing eyes.

"Better stay off the streets, my friends, at least for the time being," murmured Bishop Hugh wryly, when a deputation from the ghetto came to thank him. "Within a few days this madness will pass, never fear." Meanwhile the Bishop harbored no illusions about his flock. He

75

knew that the slightest provocation, even unintended, could undo all his good work and set the flames of hatred roaring through the city once more.

Twice more Hugh faced armed and angry mobs of Jew-baiters and twice more he forced them to back down. At Stamford and again at Northampton—both towns in his own diocese—he saved the Jewish population from massacre.

While Thomas Becket has always been a hero, Hugh of Lincoln is now largely forgotten—which is a pity, for in the whole history of the Middle Ages it would be hard to find a more engaging personality. For the Victorian writer John Ruskin, indeed, Hugh was the most attractive priest of all time. It is not hard to see why.

For many years a Carthusian solitary, Hugh was a total extrovert. Not only mobs but monarchs, too, fell victim to his fire and his charm. Throughout his life he fought for the underdog, whether Jewish or Christian. He loved small children and they loved him. He had a strange power over animals.

He began life as a Benedictine and entered the Grand Chartreuse only after some hesitation. When he presented himself, the Prior did his best to discourage the young man. "The hairshirt alone would bring the flesh off your bones," he warned, perhaps exaggerating somewhat.

Hugh, however, became a happy Carthusian, despite severe fleshly temptations which he countered by fasting even more than the Rule demanded. Appointed Procurator of the Order, with charge of the lay-brothers, he was a notable success and his fame soon spread outside the monastery walls.

It was, indirectly, the murder of Thomas Becket which brought Hugh of Avalon—as he then was—to England at the age of forty. Among his many acts of penance, Henry the Second founded a Carthusian monastery, the first in England, at Witham in Somerset. Under the first two Priors, the project made little progress and it became clear that a man of exceptional talent would be needed to save it from being stillborn. A French nobleman recommended Hugh, whose protests of his own unworthiness were over-ruled by his superiors.

When he arrived, he found the monastery buildings not even begun. What distressed him more, nothing had been given to the poor people who had been evicted to make way for them. Now came the first of Hugh's many battles for the downtrodden. Needless to say, he won. He told the King bluntly that he would not continue as Prior until the last penny of compensation had been paid.

The peasants got their cash and work on the buildings began. Soon it was at a halt, this time because Henry had not paid the bills. Hugh and two fellow-monks called on the King, who received them politely.

Hugh had decided on a tactful approach but one of his colleagues, quick-tempered Brother Girard, was in no mood to mince words.

"Whatever plans you have got for the future, whether for stopping or going on with the work, I won't be here to see them," he stormed. "You enjoy your riches—I'm going back to our desert at Chartreuse. You think you're doing us a favor just giving us bread. Well, we don't need it from you! We'd be better off on our rock in the Alps than coping with a man like you, who thinks that anything he spends on his salvation is lost!"

Hugh, acutely embarrassed at his friend's outburst, looked at the ground and waited for the royal storm to break over their heads. Henry, however, merely sat silent and pondering. Then he turned to Hugh.

"Well, my good man," he said mildly, "what about you? Are you going to leave me to enjoy my riches."

Hugh's reply was worthy of Dale Carnegie.

"No, I don't take so gloomy a view of you, Sir," he said.
"I realise that a King's life is a busy one and full of problems. It must be hard for you, sometimes, to give all the
attention you should to the things that matter for your
salvation. Nevertheless, I'm šure that with God's help
you will finish what you have begun."

Henry jumped up and embraced him.

"While I'm breathing, you shall never leave my kingdom!" he declared. "And I'll pay more attention to my
soul's needs, under your care!"

Soon the Witham monastery was completed and it
flourished. Taking the King at his word, Hugh did not
hesitate to tackle him about his neglect of Church matters and especially about his habit of leaving a diocese
vacant so that he could draw its revenues for himself.

Lincoln was a particularly scandalous example.
Spread over nine counties, it was England's largest diocese, yet it had been without a Bishop for nearly eighteen
years. When Henry, in 1186, got around to remedying
this, Hugh was the man chosen. Once again he protested
that he was unworthy; once again his Order over-ruled
him.

The diocesan Chapter, meanwhile, was no more willing to have Hugh as Bishop than he was to take on the
job. A sleek, worldly lot, the Lincoln canons had hoped
that one of their own number would be named. Henry,
however, announced that this time he was going to put
God's interests first. "You are all rich enough, already,"
he told the disappointed clerics.

It is entirely to their credit that when Hugh arrived on
the scene, they swiftly realised that he was indeed the
right man to be their Bishop. It was his humility that
convinced them: they were much taken aback to learn
that he had actually tried to dodge the appointment
which they had so ardently coveted.

Nevertheless, Hugh's poverty and simplicity tried them sorely. When, at the beginning of his reign, he travelled to Winchester to see the King, he rode along the highway with a change of clothes tied in a little bundle behind him on the horse. The canons, riding splendidly along in the rear, managed to cut the embarrassing package away from his saddle before the cheering townsfolk saw it.

From the outset Hugh made it clear that he would have no truck with the clerical pocket-lining which was so much part of the medieval Church scene. At his enthronement he shook the Archdeacon of Canterbury, who performed the ceremony, by refusing to pay him the customary honorarium.

"I shall pay for my diocese only what I pay for my mitre," he murmured sweetly, in response to the outstretched palm.

At the feast which followed the ceremony he went to the opposite extreme, for he was determined that the poor, too should be his guests. Asked how many deer should be slaughtered for venison, he told the astonished steward: "Three hundred—and more if you need them!"

From his arrival in England he had been outraged by the cruel forest laws with which the royal game were protected. The King's foresters and their agents were callous bullies who, in the words of a writer of the time, "hunt the poor as if they were wild animals and devour them as their prey." Hugh pointed out to a group of these gentry that the word "forester" sounded like the Latin *foris stare*, meaning "to stand outside."

"And that is exactly what you will do," he told them grimly. "You'll stand outside the gates of Heaven when you come to be judged."

When he actually excommunicated one of the royal foresters, Henry was not pleased. He chose to hide his displeasure, however, and a short time later asked Hugh to appoint one of his favorites to a cathedral post at Lincoln. Hugh's reply, as he must have realised, could only provoke the King to even greater wrath.

"These places are for clerics, not courtiers," he told the royal messenger. "The King does not lack means to reward his servants."

The enraged monarch sent for Hugh, who found him sitting in the grounds of Woodstock Castle sewing a bandage round a cut finger. Following Henry's orders, all present completely ignored the Bishop.

Hugh, knowing his man, refused to be put down. He looked at the bandage and then at the King.

"You know," he told Henry cheerfully, "you look exactly like your kinsfolk at Falaise."

It was a daring joke at the King's expense. Henry, through his great-grandfather, William the Conqueror, was indeed descended from a humble glove-maker in the French town. The courtiers, accustomed to the King's explosive temper, scarcely dared to breathe.

After a moment's tense silence, Henry did exactly what Hugh had expected: he threw back his head and laughed. What else could a poor monarch do, finding himself up against such a mixture of dry wit and diamond-hard integrity? With a good grace he accepted Hugh's decision in the matter of the appointment. The forester did penance, was absolved and became Hugh's friend.

If Hugh's charm could work wonders, he also had a hot temper—as he himself admitted.

"I'm very peppery at times," he confessed, "and when I'm presiding at Chapter meetings the least thing often arouses me to anger. But my canons realise that they must take me as they find me, and for that I am very grateful."

He laid great stress on the value of inner peace as

reflecting the peace of Heaven, and he was especially
glad that, despite his hot temper, his relations with the
Chapter were always happy.

"They have never opposed me in anything since I
came to live among them," he told a friend. "I don't think
that any of them doubts my affection for him, and I believe that they, too, are fond of me."

That Hugh was a boss who stuck up for his staff, nobody could doubt. "Whoever touches you touches the
pupil of my eye," he would tell them.

In an age when the diocesan clergy were often regarded as inferior to monks and hermits, and the laity as
inferior to them all, Hugh insisted that to be a Christian
was what really mattered. Love in the heart, truth on the
lips, purity in the body: these were the three things necessary for salvation. "If any one of these is lacking when a
man comes to be judged," he said, "then the very name
Christian will do him harm, for unfaithfulness is always
worse in those who profess faith."

In his attitude to women he was also well ahead of his
time. Despite his monastic background he often invited
them to dine at his table and would embrace them when
they left. "No man could ever call himself the Father of
God," he reminded them, "but a woman was made God's
Mother."

The peppery prelate's love of children was proverbial;
in playing with them his mind was freed from diocesan
cares. When a crying infant immediately broke into gur-
gles of delight on being taken into his arms, colleagues
commented on his winning way with the small-fry. Hugh
shyly admitted that, on a visit to France, one of his tiny
nephews had reacted in exactly the same way. It was the
nearest he ever came to boasting.

As a young monk in the Grand Chartreuse, he had
loved to feed birds and squirrels in his tiny garden,

where frequently they would take food from his hand. In England his favorite pet was a large swan which flew in to settle one day at Stow, a Lincolnshire village where the Bishop had a property. This fierce bird would beat off anyone who came near it—anyone but Hugh, that is. Whenever he arrived, it made a tremendous fuss, nestling up against him and spending the night in his room. Most pictures of Hugh show him with his swan.

Like so many other saints he worked frighteningly long hours, generally rising before daybreak and not eating until after nightfall. It seems unfair that, after all that fasting, he should eventually have grown fat!

He would, too, readily turn his hand to any task. When he arrived in Lincoln, he found the cathedral sadly delapidated. The new Bishop helped in the rebuilding with his own hands, working alongside the masons and carpenters. Hugh's handiwork is there still; today's visitors to Lincoln Cathedral can see St. Hugh's Choir for themselves.

Though he drove himself hard, Hugh was invariably easier on his subordinates. When consecrating a church, he would always insist that his deacon and sub-deacon should take a little food and drink first, in case they should become faint during the long ceremony.

Much of his time was, of course, spent in travelling the roads of his huge diocese, when he would usually administer Confirmation to groups of people assembled at pre-arranged points along the way. Unlike some Bishops— including several who were younger than himself—he would always dismount from his horse to administer the sacrament, lest the children present should be frightened by the stamping hooves.

On one occasion a somewhat elderly candidate came puffing and panting to the appointed spot just as Hugh and his party were pulling away. Unwilling to keep the

next group of people waiting, Hugh suggested that the
man should follow on behind and be confirmed with
them, since the place was not far distant. The old peasant
was, for some reason, unwilling to do this. Instead he
threw up his hands and, in a loud voice, called on God to
witness that if he died unconfirmed it would be all
Hugh's fault.

Hugh considered for a moment, then got down from
his mount and confirmed the old man. The ceremony
complete, he gave him a box on the ear for having delayed his reception of the sacrament until so late in life!
As one of Hugh's modern biographers remarks, the ways
of the Middle Ages were not our ways.

For the dead he had a particular affection, doubtless a
legacy of his Carthusian days, when the monks would
leave their solitary cells to say farewell to a departed
brother. He never missed a chance to conduct a funeral
and if he happened on one which was already in progress, he would invariably take over. Once, when he had a
dinner-date with the King, he kept Henry waiting while
he completed a series of burials. On another occasion,
while travelling outside his diocese, he was told that a
beggar with no-one to mourn him had been buried by the
roadside without any service. Hugh himself read the
prayers, then reported the parish priest for neglecting his
duty.

Even more striking was the care which he took of lep-
ers. A third of his income was spent on hospitals and
homes for them. He looked after the poor patients with
his own hands and would often kiss and embrace them,
refusing to be repelled by their symptoms. "Their kiss
heals my soul," he used to say.

During his lifetime Hugh was credited with many
miracles. He always refused to discuss them, nor would
he allow others to do so in his presence. He once cured a

mad sailor after the local Bishop had ridden away in terror and he healed many other diseases by laying on
hands. A young man attending Hugh's Mass became a
monk after seeing, in place of the Host, the Infant Christ
in the Bishop's hands at the Consecration.

It was said of Hugh that he was as fearless as a lion in
any danger. He proved this once more towards the end of
his life, when Henry's successor, Richard the First, tried
to force the Bishops to subsidise a foreign war. Hugh,
almost alone among his colleagues, refused on the
grounds that the tax was illegal.

Facing the irate monarch, Hugh boldly upbraided him
for this and other unjust actions, then pulled out all his
charm to calm Richard's rage. Later Richard declared:
"If all the prelates of the Church were like him, there is
not a King in Christendom who would dare to lift his
head in the presence of a Bishop."

Hugh died in London, at the age of sixty, on the evening of November 16, 1200. His body was taken to Lincoln and buried in the cathedral, in the presence of many
distinguished mourners and of the ordinary folk of the
town. The Jews were there too, sorrowing over the loss of
the protector whom they called "a true servant of the
Great God."

7

Everybody's Hero

No doubt about it, the page-boy stole the show. To begin with, the youngster was not supposed to be in the play at all. Yet suddenly there he was, moving among the actors with as much assurance as any professional, ad-libbing a part so skilfully that he made it look as though it had been written for him; his dry, topical jokes adding just the right flavor to the somewhat pedestrian script.

The Cardinal loved it and so did his guests. How the cast felt at being upstaged by a thirteen-year-old, we have not been told. Evidently they had to make the best of it, for we do know that the young comedian livened up more Christmas plays in the great palace at Lambeth.

"This child here waiting at table will prove a marvellous man," the Cardinal would often declare afterwards to the rich and famous who came to dinner. The guests, following his affectionate gaze, would glance curiously at the handsome lad with the humorous, intelligent face. John Morton, Archbishop of Canterbury and Lord Chancellor of England, was one of the shrewdest men in the land. He was not likely to be wrong. He was not wrong about Thomas More.

All his life Thomas went on joking. He joked when he was rich and famous and the King's friend. He joked in his bleak, narrow cell in the Tower of London. As all the world knows, he joked when, ill and prematurely old, he at last mounted the rickety scaffold to face the headman's axe on Tower Hill.

Like that other Thomas who became Chancellor and royal favorite, Thomas More was born in the City of London—in Milk Street, just off the same Cheapside where Becket first drew breath 380 years before. His father, John, was a successful barrister who later became a judge. Thomas was the son of his first wife, the former Alice Grainger.

It was undoubtedly from Judge More that Thomas inherited his dry sense of humor. Choosing a wife, the old gentleman observed once, was like putting a hand into a bagful of snakes and eels, with seven snakes for every eel. Nevertheless John himself made no fewer than four dips into the bag, taking his last trip to the altar when he was almost seventy.

After a spell at St. Anthony's School, not far from his home, young Thomas went into Cardinal Morton's household. It was the Cardinal who decided that he should go on to Oxford, in his judgement the proper place for a boy with a bright future ahead of him.

The life of a fifteenth-century undergraduate was nothing if not tough. Up for Mass at five, he began classes an hour later and got nothing to eat until his frugal breakfast at ten. Then it was more study until five in the afternoon, when he ate the second and last meal of the day. Latin was spoken at all times, with harsh penalties for those who lapsed into English.

Though John More was far from poor, he kept his son

miserably short of money. When Thomas needed a new
pair of shoes, he had to write home for the wherewithal.
If the youngster resented this at the time, he was grateful
later on. His poverty, he said kept him out of mischief
and made him mind his studies.

After two years of grammar, rhetoric and logic—the
traditional *trivium* of a medieval university—Thomas
came back to London to begin training for his father's
profession. Like all aspiring barristers, he was enrolled at
one of the Inns of Court, a sort of legal university to
which, even today, every member of the English Bar
must belong.

He pored over the law-books conscientiously enough
and became a competent lawyer, if not a great one. Yet
writs, statutes and cases held little magic for young,
hard-working Master More. For now, along with many
other clever young men of the time, he was gripped by a
passion for the new classical learning of the
Renaissance—a passion which was sweeping right
through Europe.

"You will ask me how I am getting on with my studies," he wrote a friend in 1501. "Excellently—nothing
could be better. I am giving up Latin and taking up
Greek. Grocyn is my teacher."

Greek, for centuries a lost language in Western
Europe, was not only the key to Plato, Aristotle and other
great minds of the pagan world; it was also the language
in which the New Testament had first reached the world
at large.

To make time for this extra study, and for his long
hours of prayer, Thomas slept only four or five hours a
night on a plank bed.

William Grocyn, his teacher, was a priest. So were the
other lifelong friends whom he made at this time: John
Colet, Thomas Linacre and Desiderius Erasmus, the

brilliant restless Dutchman from Rotterdam; all of them
enthusiasts for the new learning and keen to put the
world to rights.

With so many clerical friends around him it is scarcely
surprising that Thomas should have thought seriously
about offering himself for ordination. Though the Fran-
ciscans attracted him for a time, it was with the Carthu-
sians of London that he eventually tried his vocation. At
their suggestion he did not take vows but lived with the
monks as a sort of unofficial oblate, following as much of
the Rule as he could while completing his studies and
beginning his career at the Bar.

It took Thomas four years of prayer and self-scrutiny to
decide that the monastic life was not for him. In the
well-known words of Erasmus, he "resolved to be an
unchaste husband rather than a licentious priest."

Thomas had already been in love, at the age of sixteen,
with a girl called Elizabeth. We know that he never forgot her because he wrote a poem to her long afterwards.
The girl whom he now married, however, was not
Elizabeth but a squire's daughter from Essex called Jane
Colt. He was actually more attracted to her younger sister, but thinking it unkind to leave Jane on the shelf, he
proposed to her instead.

The marriage got off to a shaky start. Jane, who was
only seventeen, did not like London and pined for her
country home. Thomas's clever friends overawed her;
like most girls of her time, she had received little or no
education. Her husband tried to cure this defect by getting her to repeat the substance of the sermons which she
had heard in church. It is not, perhaps, surprising that
Jane did nothing but cry and wish herself dead. Finally,
in desperation, Thomas took her back home to her father.

"Use your rights and give her a good beating," was Sir
John's blunt advice. Many a Tudor husband would have
done just that, but it was not Thomas's way.

"I would rather that you used your authority," he replied mildly.

Rising to the occasion, Sir John put on so fearful a display of anger that poor Jane was glad to take refuge in her husband's arms. Pulling herself together, she became a good wife and an accomplished hostess, able to chat in simple Latin to Erasmus—of whom she became very fond—and the other cultured foreigners who came to the house. Rapidly she bore her husband a son and three daughters.

Their happiness did not last. Six years later, Jane was dead. We do not know what illness took her from her little family: possibly she died in childbirth. That her husband was heartbroken we do know from the tender epitaph which he composed for her.

Yet within a month of her funeral, Thomas More married again. His Carthusian confessor, Father John Bouge, has recorded his shock when Thomas appeared on his doorstep, late one Sunday evening, with a dispensation for the wedding next day.

His new wife, the redoubtable Alice Middleton, was a widow with a tongue as sharp as her bridegroom's wit. Unkind things have been written about Alice, and about Thomas for marrying her in such haste. His motive was, however, clear and unselfish. His four tiny children needed someone to replace the mother whom they had so tragically lost. Alice was ideally qualified and Alice was willing. So why delay matters?

That his choice proved to be an inspired one, nobody can fairly deny. Alice was not young, nor was she pretty. Thomas himself described her, somewhat ungallantly, as "neither a pearl nor a girl." To Erasmus she was "aged, blunt and rude." Another friend wrote of "the hooked beak of the harpy"—an unflattering reference to Alice's nose.

Her first husband, John Middleton, had been a down-

to-earth London merchant with no scholarly pretensions.
It may be that her new husband's friends irritated her
with their Latin conversation and their high-falutin'
ways—and Alice was never one to hide her feelings.
Whatever the reason for the animosity, Erasmus at least
seems eventually to have warmed to her. Three years
later he wrote of her more kindly, praising her as a con-
scientious housewife.

Thomas himself assures us that she was very much
more than that. Alice was that rare jewel, a stepmother
who loved her four new children as dearly as though
they were her own. Though she bore Thomas no more
sons and daughters, her own daughter, Alice junior, came
to live at the More homestead in the City.

That the family was so happy must have been in no
small measure due to Alice, for now her husband was a
busy man indeed. A rising lawyer with an expanding
practice, he was also increasingly involved in public life.
He served both as a member of Parliament and an Un-
dersheriff of the City, and he several times travelled
abroad to represent the London merchants in legal disputes with their opposite numbers in other European
countries.

Despite all these pressures, he spent long hours in
prayer, just as he had done during his four years in the
Charterhouse. Dame Alice, meanwhile, was puzzled because, instead of allowing her to see to the washing of his
shirts, he was sending them to be laundered elsewhere.
Eventually she discovered the truth. Thomas was wearing a hairshirt—one of such roughness that it left the
shirts bloodstained, and he did not want her to know.
Much disturbed, she asked his confessor to make him
throw it away, but evidently she had no success. Years
later, to Thomas's acute embarrassment, his daughter-
in-law caught sight of it when he shed his neckwear one
hot summer day.

It seems incredible that with all his other commit-
ments, he should also have found time for literary output.
Yet in 1516, during a business trip to Flanders, he wrote
Utopia, a book which gave a new word to the English
language and has excited admiration and argument down
to the present day.

Utopia—"nowhere"—is an ideal kingdom somewhere
beyond the Equator, where poverty, crime and injustice
no longer exist. It is ruled by reason, as reason was
viewed by the English humanists, and although the
rights of private property are recognised, the book ultimately recognises the rightness of Communism.

Thomas wrote *Utopia* because he was deeply grieved
by the new, unrestrained capitalism of the age: a
capitalism which make it possible for "rich men to buy
up all". He hankered after the more ordered economic
conditions of medieval times, in which monks and
monasteries had played so large a part.

To what extent is *Utopia* intended to be taken as a
serious political program and to what extent is it a fantasy
written with tongue in cheek? As a wise critic has observed, Thomas himself would almost certainly have
been unable to answer that question. Certainly it would
be wrong to take the book as representing his practical
opinion on religion and politics. Rebuking Thomas for
his deadpan jokes, a friend once told him: "You look
so sadly when you mean so merrily that many times
men doubt whether you speak in sport when you mean
good earnest." The same problem faces readers of
Utopia.

Its appearance caused a major literary stir. Within a
few years it had been translated into most European languages. Among its many admirers were, inevitably, King
Henry the Eighth and his Chancellor, Cardinal Wolsey.
Both swiftly decided that here was a talent too valuable
to be left to any law practice. Reluctantly, for he knew

the perils and pitfalls of life at Court, Thomas More found himself a member of the King's Council.

In that very same year an obscure university teacher named Martin Luther pinned his 95 theses to the church door at Wittenberg. Unlike many of his fellow-humanists, Thomas More felt no inclination to enlist under the Reformer's banner, though he was as well aware as anyone of the abuses which were rife in the Church, and as keen to see them corrected.

During the years that followed, while occupying a succession of public posts, Thomas several times wielded his pen against the new doctrines. He took on, in particular, William Tyndale, the English apostate friar whose version of the New Testament was based on Luther's teachings.

In these doctrinal battles he did not escape criticism from his own side, for there were those who felt that Master More did not always treat theological issues with due solemnity. For example, in reply to Luther's dictum that confession to a priest was unnecessary and that any friend would suffice for the purpose, Thomas observed that if a pretty woman were to hear confessions, many a man who had formerly delayed that duty would find it easy frequently to ease his conscience.

In 1521 Thomas helped King Henry, who fancied himself as a theologian, to put together a Latin work entitled *An Assertion of the Seven Sacraments*. Pope Leo the Tenth rewarded this royal effort by naming Henry "Defender of the Faith"—a title which Britain's Anglican monarchs still retain.

Despite all his public cares Thomas remained a devoted family man, always able to find time for his large and happy household. Erasmus, on a visit to his old friend, was taken into the garden to see the monkey, the rabbits, the fox, the ferret and the weasel. Every evening family and servants met for night prayers. Scripture, with a commentary, was read at meal-times. Though jokes were allowed and encouraged, cards and dice were strictly forbidden.

The children learned the Greek alphabet by shooting at the letters, for Thomas was ahead of his time in insisting that his daughters should be properly educated. Possibly he wanted to spare them and their future husbands the traumas which he had endured with poor Jane! Whatever his motives, the girls became competent scholars and in due course demonstrated their accomplishments before the King. Especially gifted was Margaret, the eldest, whose Latin style so much astonished her father's friends that they could not believe that it was a woman's work.

Margaret married William Roper, an intense young man who shortly afterwards paralysed the More household by announcing his conversion to Lutheranism. Thomas, who was genuinely fond of "Son Roper," refused to let the apostasy poison their relationship. When argument failed prayer was redoubled, and soon William was Catholic again. Much later, he wrote his father-in-law's life; to him we owe a good deal of what we know about Thomas.

In 1525 the More family moved to a grand new house by the river at Chelsea. Here, just as before, he received poor neighbors at his table and made them feel as welcome as the King—who also came to visit. Thomas himself went into the back lanes to inquire about poverty-stricken families, and gave them whatever help they needed. Whenever he learned that a local woman had gone into labor, he knelt and prayed for her until news came that she was safely delivered.

Four years later, in October, 1529, Henry appointed him Lord Chancellor in place of the disgraced Cardinal

Wolsey. Thomas, indifferent as always to power and
wealth, continued to sing in the church choir on Sundays, dressed in a surplice.

Everything in his life seemed set fair, yet already the
storm which would destroy him was visible on the hori-
zon. Henry, troubled at the lack of a male heir and in-
fatuated by Anne Boleyn, was having scruples—real or
induced—about his marriage to Catherine of Aragon, who
had been his brother Arthur's widow. Wolsey had fallen
precisely because he had failed to persuade Rome to
annul the marriage. Henry felt that the Cardinal, for reasons of his own, had not tried hard enough.

Thomas believed the marriage valid, though he re-
frained from making any public statement of his opinion
even when asked for one by Parliament. Instead he con-
centrated on clearing the backlog of judicial work which
Wolsey had left undone, so earning the gratitude of liti-
gants who had waited years for a hearing. He himself told
how he worked on until, one day, he called the next case
"and there was none."

Early in 1530 the King made a fresh approach to Rome.
Tactlessly, the delegation included the Earl of Wiltshire,
Anne Boleyn's father! It did not succeed, nor did a Government petition which Thomas refused to sign. Very
well, said Henry. If Rome would not do his will, he
would replace Rome's authority with his own.

In February, 1531, he forced the Bishops to acknowledge him as "Supreme Head of the Church of England,"
allowing them the conscience-salving clause—"as far as
the law of Christ allows". Only John Fisher, Bishop of
Rochester, spoke out boldly against this surrender without a fight. "The fort is betrayed even by them that
should have defended it," he declared.

Thomas, greatly distressed, tried to resign his post.
Henry persuaded him to remain, promising him that he

would not be pressed to take up a public position on the King's "Great Matter"—as the annulment question was called.

It was an impossible situation, as Thomas must have known, for he had no illusions about his royal master. Once, at Chelsea, his son-in-law had marvelled to see the monarch, his arm round Thomas's shoulders, walking with him up and down the garden in affectionate conversation. "Son Roper, I may tell thee, I have no cause to be proud of that," said Thomas afterward, "for if my head would win him a castle in France, it should not fail to go."

Now he we was forced openly to defy Henry, with much more than a castle in France at stake. Early in 1532, as a fresh step in his takeover, Henry proposed to forbid the clergy to prosecute heretics or to hold any meeting without his permission. He also moved to stop a tax which the Bishops traditionally paid to the Holy See.

All these measures Thomas opposed, to Henry's predictable chagrin. On May 16, pleading illness, he was allowed to resign his office as Chancellor. In fact he had been suffering from chest pains, no doubt induced by the stress of his situation.

"We may not look at our pleasure to go to Heaven in feather beds," he had often told his family. "It is not the way. For Our Lord himself went there with great pain and many tribulations. The servant may not look to be in better case than the master."

Always ready for misfortune when it should come, he faced poverty with the utmost cheerfulness. Calling his household together, he explained in detail, and with much humor, how their standard of living would be affected. If the worst came to the worst, he added, smiling, "we may yet go a-begging together and hoping that for pity some good folk will give us their charity."

Knowing that the ex-Chancellor's generosity had left him with little to fall back on, the Bishops and Abbots of England collected a sum which would have kept the Mores in luxury for a considerable time. Thomas would not accept a penny. Yet he and his family were now so poor that they could no longer afford coal fires. Each night they used to gather a big pile of ferns and burn them in Thomas's bedroom. Having warmed themselves, off they went to bed.

For eighteen months. Thomas lived quietly, dividing his time between prayer, study and writing. Meanwhile, in the world outside, events were moving rapidly toward a crisis.

In January, 1533, Henry went through a form of marriage with Anne Boleyn. Four months later the Archbishop of Canterbury, Thomas Cranmer, declared their union valid. On Whit Sunday, June 1, Anne was crowned Queen in Westminster Abbey. Thomas More was invited to the ceremony but did not go.

The More family always believed that in that moment, Thomas virtually signed his own death-warrant. There is no direct evidence that Anne goaded the King into action against him but the suspicion is strong, for she was certainly arrogant and vindictive toward others.

The first sinister move was an attempt to implicate Thomas in the case of Elizabeth Barton, the "Holy Maid of Kent," a demented young woman who had prophesied against the King. Though Elizabeth was executed, Henry eventually let the case against Thomas drop; but his salary as a King's Councillor was stopped, plunging him even deeper into poverty.

Soon afterward, the bluff Duke of Norfolk tried to give Thomas a good-natured warning of the danger which faced him.

"By the Mass, Master More," he declared, "it is perilous striving with princes. And therefore I would wish you somewhat to incline to the King's pleasure. For by God's body, Master More, *indignatio principis mors est*" (the wrath of the King is death).

"Is that all, my lord?" Thomas replied. "Then in good faith is there no more difference between your Grace and me, but that I shall die today and you tomorrow."

In July, 1533, the Pope excommunicated Henry and declared his union with Anne invalid. Eight months later he confirmed the validity of his marriage to Catherine.

Henry replied with the Act of Succession, which required the King's subjects to take an oath recognising his offspring by Anne as heirs to the throne. To this he added clauses declaring that his marriage to Catherine was no true marriage, that his union with Anne was a true marriage, and repudiating the rights of "any foreign authority, prince or potentate"

From the beginning Thomas had feared that the King would make just such a move. "God give grace, son, that these matters within a while be not confirmed with oaths," he had said to Roper as soon as he heard of the impending union with Anne. Now his fear had come true.

On Low Sunday, April 12, 1534, Thomas More was summoned to Lambeth to take the Oath of Succession. He refused.

The next four days he spent in the custody of the Abbot of Westminster. Meanwhile Archbishop Cranmer, one of the Oath Commissioners, tried to work out a compromise which would save both Thomas and John Fisher, who had also stuck to his guns. Cranmer did not succeed.

On Friday, April 17, Thomas was again called before the Commissioners and again asked to take the Oath. Persisting in his refusal, he was immediately taken to the Tower.

During the fifteen months which he spent there, his
greatest trial was undoubtedly the inability of his
family—and especially of his wife and of his dearly-
beloved Margaret—to understand why he had to make so
great a sacrifice. When Margaret tried to dissuade him
from his chosen course, he smiled sadly and called her
"Mistress Eve."

Where Margaret could employ sophisticated argument, poor, broken-hearted Dame Alice had only her
sharp tongue to rely upon.

"I marvel that you," she said, "that have been always
hitherto taken for so wise a man, will now so play the fool
to lie here in this close, filthy prison, and be content thus
to be shut up amongst mice and rats, when you might be
abroad at your liberty."

"I pray thee, good Mistress Alice, tell me one thing,"
he asked, when she had done.

"What is that?"

"Is not this house as nigh Heaven as my own?"

Alice, in no mood for smart answers, snorted in disgust.
Suppose, persisted Thomas, he were to lie dead and
buried for seven years and then return alive to Chelsea.
Would he not find a new owner settled in his home?
"What cause have I then to like such a house," he con-
cluded with a grin, "as would so soon forget its master?"

In his cell Thomas found at last the close union with
God which as a young man he had sought in the Charterhouse. "Me thinketh that God maketh me a wanton,
and setteth me on his lap and dandleth me," he said,
evidently referring to a mystical experience.

It seems that even before his arrest he had regretted
having turned aside from the monastic vocation. When
Margaret was distressed at the cell's bareness and nar-
rowness, her father told her that were it not for his family

responsibilities "I would not have failed long ere this to have closed myself in as strait a room, and straiter too."

It was an added cruelty of the time that prisoners, as well as having to provide their own food, were also forced to pay a weekly rent for their "lodgings." Thomas, as a commoner, was charged fifteen shillings. John Fisher, who ranked as a lord, had to pay a pound.

Though prisoners for more than a year, Thomas More and John Fisher were never allowed to meet face to face. Letters were sometimes smuggled, however, and in one of them Thomas announced that he was sending the Bishop a "present" of 2,000 pounds. Evidently this is one of Thomas's jokes, though the point of it has been lost. Perhaps he included a drawing of a money-bag with the sum written on it.

Before pen and ink were finally taken from him, Thomas employed them more seriously on *A Dialogue of Comfort Against Tribulation*, written for fellow-victims of persecution. He also composed a treatise on the Passion of Christ.

Throughout his life, even in times of health and prosperity, Thomas More had treated death as an ever-present reality. Perhaps that was easier in his day than in ours. Medical science, still in its infancy, had made little progress in conquering disease. Honorable men could be killed at the King's will. "We never ought to look toward death as a thing far off," he had written, "considering that although he make no haste towards us, yet we never cease ourselves to make haste toward him."

Now, more than ever before, death was a close neighbor. From his cell window he watched John Houghton, Prior of the dear, familiar London Charterhouse, dragged out on a hurdle with three other priests to be hanged, drawn and quartered at Tyburn.

"Dost thou not see, Meg," he observed to Margaret, "that these blessed fathers be now as cheerfully going to their deaths as bridegrooms to a marriage?" If his captors had let him see them in the hope of intimidating him, they failed.

When Dame Alice came once more, this time to tempt him with the prospect of longevity, he met her with his customary humor.

"And how long, my Alice," he asked, "should I be able to enjoy this life?"

"A full twenty years," she replied, "if God so wills."

"Do you wish me, then," retorted her husband, "to exchange eternity for twenty years? Nay, good wife, you do not bargain very skilfully. If you had said some thousands of years you would have said something, but yet what would that be compared with eternity?"

Though ready to face martyrdom if it came, he did not feel any duty to rush headlong into it. For this reason he steadfastly declined to say why he had refused the Oath. Thomas More was much too clever a lawyer to hand his opponents their case on a plate. Even when Henry, by the Act of Supremacy, formally made himself Head of the Church of England, he refused point-blank to express any opinion.

Thomas Cromwell, the King's principal secretary, has often been painted as a crafty villain bent on Thomas More's destruction. He appears so in Robert Bolt's superb play, *A Man For All Seasons*. In fact there is evidence that he liked the ex-Chancellor and would have saved him if he could. Cromwell was, however, an efficient civil servant with a job to do. Exasperated by his silence, he told Thomas that his stubborness was making other men stiff-necked. Thomas replied, truthfully, that he had given advice in the matter to no-one.

"I do nobody any harm, I say none harm, I think none

harm," he said. "And if this be not enough to keep a man alive, in good faith I long not to live."

In May, 1535, Pope Paul the Third created John Fisher a Cardinal. King Henry, he believed, would not execute a member of the Sacred College. Told of the honor, Henry cruelly joked that by the time the red hat arrived from Rome, the new Cardinal would no longer have a head on which to put it. He kept his promise. On June 22, the sick old man, almost too frail to stand unaided, was beheaded on Tower Hill.

Nine days later, Thomas's trial opened in Westminster Hall. Whe he made his appearance, those who knew him were shocked to see how weak and ill he, too, had become. Already his property had been forfeited to the Crown and Alice had been forced to sell her clothes to buy him food and other necessities.

The prosecution tried to prove that he had, at various times, opposed the Act of Supremacy, and that in any case he had failed to uphold it as a good subject should. Thomas declared once more that he had at all times kept silence on the subject. Conducting his own defence, he took his stand on the common law maxim *qui tacet, consentire videtur*—that silence implies consent. In other words, nobody had the right to assume that because he had refused to give an opinion, he was necessarily opposed to the Act. In the absence of other evidence, the presumption was to the contrary.

It was a lawyer's stratagem, naked and unashamed. Even now, Thomas was not going to lay his head upon the block without a fight.

In the end he was found guilty, as he knew he must be. Sir Thomas Audley, his successor as Chancellor, was an old friend. It was his duty to pass sentence and he tried to get it over quickly.

To everyone's surprise, Thomas, after years of silence,

claimed a convicted prisoner's right to speak. What need
was there of silence now? Bluntly he told the court that
the Act of Supremacy was directly repugnant to the law
of God, to the law of the Church, and to the law of England as laid down in Magna Carta and elsewhere.

"No more may this Realm of England refuse obedience to the See of Rome," he declared, "than might a
child refuse obedience to his own natural father."

The sentence was that he be hanged, drawn and quartered. Henry commuted it to beheading on Tower Hill.
Perhaps this was for the sake of their old friendship;
more probably, because he feared a public demonstra-
tion if the popular ex-Chancellor were dragged through
the streets of Tyburn.

Thomas's last letter, to Margaret, was written with a
piece of charcoal. "Farewell, my dear child, and pray for
me," he told her, "and I shall for you and all your friends,
that we may meet merrily in Heaven."

He mounted the scaffold at 9 a.m. on Tuesday, July 6,
1535. "I pray you, Master Lieutenant," he asked, "see
me safe up, and for my coming down let me shift for
myself."

It appears that no priest was present, nor—perhaps by
his own wish—was any member of his family. In a brief
speech he asked the crowd to pray for him, as he would
pray for them elsewhere. He died, he said, "the King's
good subject but God's first."

Even as he placed his head on the block there was a
final joke, the most famous of all. "This hath not offended
the King," he murmured, laying his long beard aside.
The headsman, who had first asked and received his forgiveness, decapitated him with a single blow.

Tradition says that when news of the execution was
brought, Henry was playing cards with Anne Boleyn.

"You are the cause of this man's death," he told her. Then he left her and shut himself up alone.

It was not, of course, for his sense of humor that Thomas was canonised with John Fisher four centuries afterwards. Nor was it merely because of his heroic death. Even had Henry left him in peace, he might well have been numbered as a confessor in the calendar of saints.

Today he is everybody's hero because he died, not simply for the Catholic religion, but for the right of each man to follow his own conscience to the end. That is why even cynical old Jonathan Swift called him "the person of the greatest virtue this kingdom ever produced". It is also why Thomas More, the man for all seasons, steadfastly refused to judge or to condemn those whose consciences directed a course different from his own.

8

The Brave Wife of York

John Clitherow was a kindly man, except when he was drunk. Then he could become loud-mouthed and offensive. He was drunk now, and pitching into the Roman Catholics.

"Don't be deceived by them, friends," he roared. "They'll fast, pray and give alms more than any of us Protestants, true enough. Yet for all that, they are just as bad as we are, if not worse." Gloatingly he proceeded to enumerate scandals involving local Catholics, each more lurid than the last, each manufactured from his own beer-sodden imagination.

One or two of his fellow-guests made half-hearted attempts to change the subject, but there was no deflecting John from his theme. Feet shuffled in embarrassment as everyone tried to avoid looking at the one Catholic in the room. Pretty young Margaret Clitherow stood pale and tense, not a muscle of her face moving, as she listened to her husband tearing her religion and her friends to shreds.

At last Margaret could bear it no longer. She burst into

tears. In a moment the women were round her, begging
her not to take any notice of a husband too drunk to know
what he was saying. The men, ashamed of their earlier
timidity, pitched loudly into John. Didn't he know better
than to hurt his wife in public that way?

It took John's befogged brain a couple of moments to
comprehend the damage which he had done. Full of
bleary remorse, he muttered that of course, he did not
include Margaret in his anti-Catholic strictures. "I've
always said that a man couldn't wish for a better wife,"
he protested. "In fact I've only got two complaints
against her. She fasts too much and she won't go to
church with me!"

This distressing little episode, which could so easily
have happened at a modern cocktail party, actually took
place in the ancient city of York one evening four hundred years ago. Though he was married to a saint, and
though his own brother and at least one of his sons became a priest, John Clitherow never did change his mind
about the Catholic Church. Not even his wife's terrible
martyrdom sixteen years after their marriage could
shake John from his comfortable Protestantism.

Margaret herself had grown up a conforming member
of the Church of England, though her father, Thomas
Middleton, remembered the old days and in his will left
sums of money to his servants "to pray for me."

In life, however, Thomas minded his wax-chandler's
business and attended Divine Service on Sundays, and it
never entered Margaret's head to do otherwise. When
Thomas died, she was still only eleven. A mere four
months later, her mother married again.

Margaret's new stepfather was a young innkeeper
named Henry May, a social climber determined to be
somebody in York. Marrying a well-to-do widow like
Jane Middleton was a step on the way up. It was Henry

who arranged Margaret's own marriage in July, 1571, to John Clitherow, a widower with two little sons of his own.

At fifteen years old, Margaret Clitherow found herself with a home and a staff of servants to run as well as two step-children to care for—responsibility enough, you may think, for a girl who had scarcely left her own childhood behind her. Yet that was not all. In addition to her household duties, Margaret had also to manage the butcher's shop which occupied the ground-floor front of the house in the Shambles. In future years she grew to hate the work; she begged John to close the shop down and concentrate on the wholesale side of the business. In the meantime she plied the knife and the chopper dutifully, and quickly made a name for herself as a shrewd and efficient shopkeeper.

Obedient as she was to her husband, Margaret was nevertheless the stronger character by far. Alert and vivacious, she threw herself whole-heartedly into everything that she did and she expected others to do the same. Servants who skimped their work soon learned to fear the young mistress's sharp tongue. Though she strove later on to curb this formidable organ, she never wholly succeeded.

Exactly how Margaret became a Catholic we will never know for certain, though we can make a reasonable guess. In the winter of 1569 the Earls of Northumberland and Westmorland had led a Northern rebellion whose object was to free Mary, Queen of Scots, and gain toleration for the Catholic religion in England. Though never actually attacked, York was for a time effectively under siege: heavily barricaded, crowded with soldiers and short of food.

For all her Yorkshire sharpness, Margaret had a gentle heart. When the rebellion failed, she surely pitied the hundreds of men hanged in reprisal and the families they left behind. From every town and village which had supported it, victims were taken out and strung up brutally.

Thomas Percy, the dashing Earl of Northumberland, had been the driving force behind the whole enterprise. He suffered his inevitable fate on the Pavement at York, only a hundred yards from Margaret's shop. When he laid his head on the block that August day in 1572, Margaret may well have been in the crowd that marvelled at his bravery, as he faced the axe without a twitch or a tremor. She may, too, have craned forward to hear his dying declaration: "If I had a thousand lives, I would give them up for the Catholic faith."

In that same year, 1572, Margaret herself became a mother. Perhaps her pregnancy, and the hours spent feeding little Henry, gave her more time for thought than she had ever known. Events had certainly given her much to think about.

Thirty-five years before, in her father's time, another, similar rebellion—the Pilgrimage of Grace—had been put down by Henry the Eighth with a brutality to match that lately shown by his daughter. Then, too, men from the rebel areas of the North had been hanged by the hundred. Thomas Percy and his followers must have known in advance the price of their own failure.

Yet even after this second wave of bloodshed, the Catholic faith lived on; indeed, it seemed to be stronger than ever. To keep the unruly Northerners down, Elizabeth sent the Earl of Huntingdon, a sour-faced Puritan tyrant. Arriving in York, he smelt Popery in the very air. Prayers for the dead, rosary beads and other Romish practices were in full swing. The Yorkshire people were showing, he reported bitterly, "great stiffness to retain their wonted errors."

What was the Catholic religion that men should be so ready to die for it—and to die cheerfully too? Why did so many of the older people around her still quietly mourn the loss of the Mass? Why had the North of England never really been Protestant at heart?

Questions like this must have raced through Margaret's head hour by hour as she cradled her infant son in her arms. Soon after Thomas Percy's execution, Margaret Clitherow began to receive instruction in the Catholic faith.

In sixteenth-century York, instruction was not hard to find. Not far from her home in the Shambles lived Dr. Edward Vavasour and his wife, Dorothy; both were Catholics and both were much loved by their neighbors for their kindness to the sick and the poor. It was in their home, by a priest unknown, that the beautiful young butcher's wife was taught the old religion and reconciled to the Church.

The times were dangerous for a young woman to be seen hurrying through the narrow streets—so many of them still there today—to a house notorious as a centre of Catholic activity. Resourceful as always, Margaret provided herself with an excuse. As an adjunct to her husband's medical practice, Dorothy Vavasour ran a sort of maternity home. Margaret, whose versatility was known to all, pretended on each of her visits that she was going to the Vavasours to act as midwife to a lady in labor.

As a Catholic, Margaret found that the faith was indeed flourishing. As so often before in the Church's history, persecution had had exactly the opposite effect from that which the persecutors intended. Converts like herself were coming over to Rome by the hundred. Weaker Catholics, far from being intimidated, were strengthened. Each year newly-ordained priests slipped secretly into England after their studies abroad, all of them prepared for a brief ministry and a cruel death at the end of it.

Converts are noted for their enthusiasm and York had no more enthusiastic convert than Margaret Clitherow. Morning, noon and night she worked to spread the faith among her neighbors. Since no fewer than eleven butchers' wives were charged with the offence of recusancy— refusing to attend the Anglican church—we may reasonably assume that she had a fair measure of success!

Among the eleven was, of course, Margaret herself. She served her first term in jail from August, 1577, to June, 1578, spending the whole ten months in a wing of York Castle especially reserved for recusants. About the size of her family at this time, we are not sure: in addition to her stepsons she certainly had two children of her own, Henry and Anne, and she may already have given birth to her third child, a son whose name has not come down to us.

Keenly as she felt the separation from her family, Margaret found prison a joyful experience. In York Castle, as in other prisons of the time, priests and layfolk lived the life of a religious community, each with its own Superior and its own Rule. They prayed together, they studied the Scriptures together, they read the *Imitation of Christ* and other spiritual books, and discussed them afterwards. Because jailers could be easily bribed, priests slipped in and out of the Castle, bringing Mass and the Sacraments to those inside.

Margaret herself called prison "a most happy and profitable school" and it is easy to see why. When she first went there, she was a hot-head, loudly proclaiming that she, Margaret Clitherow, would forsake husband, life and all rather than return to the damnable state of Protestantism. Life inside taught her many things, among them that courage and perseverance were the gift of God, whose grace she would need constantly if she were to remain true to her resolve.

So much joy did she find there, and so much spiritual growth, that release actually made her unhappy. "I fear God saw something in me for which I was unworthy to continue among them," she said wistfully, longing for the companionship of the recusant wing. In other ways, too, her time there had been profitable. Intelligent and articulate though she was, Margaret had never previously been taught to read and write. Now she could do both, and she had learned Latin in the bargain.

Returning from her first term, she immediately set up a hiding-place where Mass could be said secretly. The room itself was in a next-door neighbor's house, with the entrance in the Clitherow residence.

Did John Clitherow know of the room's existence? It is hard to see how he could have failed to do so. Nevertheless he manfully kept silent, allowing his wife to continue on her dangerous way and paying the fines frequently imposed for her absence from church. Poor John deserves a word of credit, and perhaps a little sympathy too. He must have needed to bite hard when Margaret gaily told him, after some business setback, that fewer goods meant fewer obstacles between him and God. And was he really deceived when, on the pretext of attending a wedding, she slipped away for a whole day to make a retreat in the country?

Although her fasting continued to worry him—she frequently took only one meal—John could not have failed to notice the new serenity which the years in prison had brought to her. He must have marvelled, too, at her readiness to share even the most unpleasant household tasks with the servants—including those which no other wife of her class would have touched. "God forbid that I should will any to do that in my house which I would not willingly do myself first," she declared cheerfully.

It was Margaret's delight to wait on others, even those whom the world might see as her social inferiors. When her little group of Catholic friends met for Mass, it was invariably she who served breakfast afterwards.

During her third term of imprisonment, in 1583, Margaret had seen her confessor, Father William Hart, dragged out of York Castle on a hurdle to be hanged at the Knavesmire a mile away. Yet in the following year, while still under house arrest, she secretly sent young Henry abroad to be educated for the priesthood.

Even as the youngster settled to his new life, authority was tightening its grip on the Catholics at home. In the wake of the Throckmorton plot—an attempt to replace Elizabeth with Mary, Queen of Scots—Parliament ordered all Jesuits and seminary priests to leave the kingdom within forty days. Students for the priesthood were to return to England.

At this point Henry May, Margaret's stepfather, re-enters the story. In January, 1586, ambitious Henry achieved his long-awaited goal: he was elected Lord Mayor of York. A stepdaughter like Margaret was clearly an acute embarrassment to a man in his position. Not only was she a notorious Catholic, she was also training a son for the priesthood in flagrant defiance of the law.

Two months later, on March 10, Margaret's home was raided. If Henry May was indeed behind the raid, his intention was probably to frighten Margaret into apostasy—he, who should have known her so well! It is unlikely that he wished her dead, or foresaw the terrible outcome.

The Sheriff's men found Margaret busy about the house. Though expecting them hourly, she had made up her mind to carry on normally. Upstairs in his secret chamber, the priest heard them barging through the shop and made a swift getaway. An armed ruffian, bursting into a downstairs room, found a school lesson in progress. The pupils were Margaret's children and some others belonging to friends; the teacher was a Catholic scholar whom Margaret had hired for the purpose.

By threatening one of the youngsters the raiders swiftly discovered the priest's hiding-place—though not, of course, the priest. Before long the same terrified child had spilled out a list of the people whom he had seen at Mass there.

Everyone in the house, the children and John Clitherow included, was locked up for the night in various prisons around the city. Two days later, Margaret was informed that for the offence of harboring and maintaining a priest she would be prosecuted with the full rigor of the law. If the intention was to frighten her, it failed.

"I wish I had something to give you for this good news," she told the messenger with a laugh. "Wait, take this fig—I have nothing better."

This happy mood continued throughout the morning. Chatting to a friend, Anne Tesh, she joked: "We are so merry together that I fear we may risk losing the merit of our imprisonment." Looking out of a window at other Catholic prisoners, she told Anne that she was going to make them laugh too—and she made a pair of gallows with her fingers.

Margaret was going to suffer the death penalty, of that she was certain. Even before her arrest, a priest friend had warned her to prepare her neck for the rope.

When the court hearing began, however, it soon became clear that humane Mr. Justice Clench was not at all keen to hang this pretty but misguided young woman. The prosecution case did not, after all, amount to much.

It should not be too difficult to steer the jury towards an acquittal.

Before there could be an acquittal, however, there must first be a trial, and before there could be a trial the accused must enter a plea of not guilty. This, to Clench's astonishment, Margaret refused to do. Indeed, she refused to enter any plea at all.

"How will you be tried?" he asked her. It was a formal question, put to all prisoners charged with felony.

"Having made no offence, I need no trial," retorted Margaret, looking him straight in the eye.

Patiently at first, then with mounting exasperation, Clench and his colleagues tried to extract the correct reply, that she consented to be tried "by God and the country." Margaret remained obstinate.

"I will be tried by none but by God and your own consciences," she declared.

By every means in their power they tried to shake her. They wheedled, shouted and cajoled. They even employed brutal shock tactics, bringing in two ruffians dressed in Mass vestments to fool around with chalices and unconsecrated hosts. Still Margaret was unmoved. Clench, seriously worried, now came as near as he dared to promising her an acquittal.

"You need not fear this kind of trial" he coaxed, "for I do not believe that the jury can find you guilty upon the slender evidence of a child."

It was no good. Margaret Clitherow would not cooperate. Didn't the stupid creature know what they would do to her if she kept this up? Very well, then she must be told or at least warned that she was risking a terrible penalty. Without spelling it out, Clench told her: "We must proceed by law against you, which will condemn you to a sharp death for want of trial."

"God's will be done," replied Margaret, with all her usual cheerfulness. "I thank God I may suffer any death for this good cause."

The jury would not, Margaret was convinced, bring in a verdict of not guilty. Whatever Clench and Henry May might want, other and more powerful men had already decided her fate. The jurors had their orders; they would hang her as a warning to all other Catholic woman that their sex would offer them no protection if they, too, fell foul of the new law. She was not prepared to let her death rest on their consciences.

She guessed, also, that the prosecution would not rely solely on the evidence of a single boy. Her own children would be brought in to give evidence against her and she would not allow that to happen. Nor would she risk the betrayal of Catholic friends that a trial would inevitably bring.

Still unwilling to sentence her, Clench sent her back to jail for the night to think over her position. Next morning he tried yet again to coax a plea from her.

"We see no reason why you should refuse," he urged, "here be but small witness against you."

"Indeed," retorted Margaret dryly, "I think you have no witnesses against me but children, whom with an apple and a rod you may make to say what you will."

To his credit Clench did not give up even now. He hinted that even should the verdict go against her, she might still be shown mercy. Margaret was unmoved.

Goaded by an impatient colleague at his side, the defeated judge at last pronounced the terrible sentence reserved for those who stood "mute of malice." She must be stripped naked, laid down on the ground and left for three days with as much weight upon her as she was able to bear. During this time she would be fed only a little barley bread and puddle water. On the third day she would be pressed to death, her hands and feet tied to posts and a sharp stone under her back.

She could still escape the sentence, Clench told her, if only she would see sense and plead. He begged her to think of her husband and children.

"I would to God my husband and children might suffer with me for so good a cause," Margaret replied calmly.

Poor John Clitherow, when he heard the news, wept so bitterly that blood gushed from his nose. "Will they kill my wife?" he cried. "Let them take all I have and save her. She is the best wife in England, and the best Catholic also."

Even as he spoke, his twelve-year-old daughter, Anne, was suffering ill-treatment in another prison for refusing to attend the Anglican service. Clearly Anne was her mother's daughter.

Since there was some possibility that Margaret might be pregnant, Clench ordered ten days' delay in the carrying out of the sentence—much to the annoyance of Huntingdon's Council in the North, who could not wait to make an example of her. Clench himself then left York, having business elsewhere. Margaret Clitherow must have troubled his sleep for many nights to come.

So eager were the councillors to kill Margaret that in the event she was spared the three-day preliminary pressing which the sentence prescribed. With the question of her pregnancy still apparently unresolved, she was told that she would die on Friday, March 25,—the day on which the judge's prohibition expired. Once more she thanked God.

Though she looked forward to a martyr's crown, Margaret never trusted to her own strength. More than once

she had seen good men and women suffer grievously for
the faith, only to give way and apostatise in the end.
During her remaining days on earth she fasted and
prayed constantly.

When the last night came, she remarked wistfully to
her cell-mate that she would have welcomed a friend's
company to encourage her. Mrs. Yoward, a kind-hearted
Protestant woman, had been thrown into prison with her
husband for debt. Now she stayed up for part of the
night, kneeling beside Margaret in prayer.

When the Sheriff's men came for her, Margaret was
dressed and ready. Though she had prayed until three in
the morning, she had also taken a few hours' rest, part of
it stretched out beside the glowing embers in the hearth.

Margaret Clitherow walked to her execution with ribbons in her hair, just as she had once walked to church as
a bride. Her hat she had sent to her husband as a sign that
she recognised his authority to the last; her shoes and
stockings she sent to Anne in hope that she should walk
in the path that her mother had chosen.

And so she walked barefoot, handing out money to the
watching crowd, everyone marvelling at the radiance of
her face. She looked, indeed, as happy as any bride on
that March morning.

In a building known as the Tolbooth everything was
ready for the hideous deed: the heavy door, the sharp
stone, the weights that would crush her ribs until they
burst from her body. A group of beggars, men and
women, stood waiting—ragged executioners, hired for a
few pence.

Dying for the Catholic faith, Margaret had gladly allowed the Protestant Mrs. Yoward to pray for her. She
had even humored, up to a point, an eccentric Puritan
minister who had visited her in prison and who had done

his inept best to save her life. Now her tormentors urged
her to pray with them. Illiterate for most of her thirty
years, she replied in words of marble:

"I will not pray with you and you shall not pray with
me; neither will I say Amen to your prayers, nor shall you
to mine."

With victory in sight, Margaret Clitherow was not to
pressured into any action which might be interpreted as
weakness or compromise.

From the first she had been appalled at the thought
that she was to die naked before the eyes of men; it was
the part of the sentence which had shocked and distressed her most. This humiliation, too, she was spared,
being allowed to change from her gown into a short linen
dress which she had made especially for her martyrdom.
It had strings on the sleeves with which her hands were
now tied to the posts. Margaret had sewed them there
willingly; indeed they were her idea, for she considered
it an honor to die in the same attitude as Our Lord.

When they laid the weights upon her, she said: "Jesu,
Jesu, Jesu, have mercy on me." Those were her last
words. Death was a quarter of an hour in coming.

Twelve years later an Essex Catholic named Jane
Wiseman was arrested just as Margaret had been. Knowing Margaret's story, she followed her example and received the same sentence. Unlike Margaret, Jane lived
close to London. When Queen Elizabeth heard about the
case, she rebuked the judges for their cruelty and ordered that the woman should not die.

9

A Jesuit Pimpernel

On a June morning in 1579, while Margaret Clitherow was quietly running her Mass-centre in York, a jewel merchant in the French port of St. Omer received a letter from a colleague urging him to come at once to London and market his wares. Four days later, accompanied by his servant, the merchant set sail. The two men landed at Dover on June 25, before daybreak.

The "merchant" was Edumnd Campion, an English Jesuit returning to his homeland after long years overseas. His servant was Ralph Emerson, a lay-brother; the colleague, Robert Persons, their Superior, who had crossed the English Channel ahead of them disguised as a swashbuckling soldier. It was a disguise which suited the ebullient Father Robert very well.

Spies abroad had warned Queen Elizabeth and her agents that the Jesuits were coming. The ports were closely watched. Yet Edmund and Ralph slipped safely through the net just as their Superior had done, though not before they had been thoroughly interrogated by the Mayor of Dover himself. At first the Mayor was suspici-

ous; for a terrible moment they feared that he would
order their arrest. In the end, however, he was satisfied
and let them go. Robert, they learned later, had passed
through the official inspection with much joking and
back-slapping.

In London Edmund, alias "Mr. Edmunds," found a
lodging at the home of a rich Catholic named George
Gilbert, one of a group of laymen pledged to work for the
faith in England. To this group he brought a blessing
from the Pope. Then he set about "marketing his
wares"—bringing Mass and the Sacraments to Catholics
all over the land.

While his enemies sought him everywhere, he moved
among them fearlessly, constantly changing his identity,
making new converts to the faith and rallying the faint-
hearted. For Catholics news that Father Campion was
among them brought tremendous excitement; for here
was not merely a brave and holy priest—there were
many of those in Elizabeth's England—but a master of
the English tongue whose works, written on the run, bril-
liantly defended the faith in the teeth of the State propaganda machine.

Like Margaret Clitherow, Edmund Campion grew up
a practising Anglican—indeed, he seemed marked out to
become a leader of the official Protestant Church. The
son of a London bookseller, he was given an Oxford
scholarship at fifteen and became one of the university's
most noted Latin orators. At seventeen he was already a
Fellow of St. John's College and the center of a devoted
crowd of pupils. They packed into his lectures, they aped
his tricks of speech, his mannerisms and his clothes; they
even called themselves "Campionists."

During a royal visit to Oxford, his skill in debate
deeply impressed the Queen. Afterwards William Cecil,
her righthand man, promised Edmund his patronage; so

too did her favorite, the Earl of Leicester. Yet, despite all this success, Edmund Campion was a troubled man.

It is probable that in 1568, when he was ordained a deacon of the Church of England, Edmund was already having serious doubts about his Anglicanism. Poring over the Fathers of the Church only made Rome's authority seem more certain. He sought the advice of an Oxford colleague, Tobie Matthew, an expert in patristic studies. How, asked Edmund, did Tobie reconcile his deep knowledge of the Father's with his Anglican profession?

"If I believed them as well as read them," replied the patrologist, "you would have reason to ask." Tobie lived to become Archbishop of York.

Edmund's Popish sympathies became known just as the Government, realising that the old religion was gathering strength rather than losing it, ordered a general tightening-up of anti-Catholic measures. His days at Oxford, Edmund realised, were numbered. On the one hand, a Catholic friend was writing to him from the seminary at Douai, urging him to come over to France and study for the priesthood; on the other, he was being pressed to show his loyalty to the State Church by preaching a well-publicised sermon at Paul's Cross in London.

Edmund did neither thing; instead he left Oxford and went to Dublin to help set up a university there. Though his work in that direction was unsuccessful—not until after his death did Trinity College become a fact—his Celtic sojourn did have one tangible result: a short *History of Ireland,* which he composed during his hours of leisure. It contains the following observation on the Irish as a people:

> Clear men they are of skin and hue, but of themselves
> careless and bestial. Their women are well favored, clear
> colored, fair headed, big and large, suffered from infancy

to grow at will, nothing curious (careful) of their feature
and proportion of body.

Though he gives due praise to Irish holiness and aus-
terity, he adds that when they are lewd, they are very
lewd indeed. His book did not find favor in Ireland.

During his Dublin period Edmund was still officially
an Anglican and an excommunicate from the Church of
Rome, though thoroughly a Catholic at heart. It was not a
happy situation and he suffered much from self-loathing
and remorse. He seems to have been hoping that in England the tide would turn once more in the Church's
favor and that he might enjoy an honorable career as a
Catholic layman.

In 1570 Pope Pius the Fifth excommunicated Queen
Elizabeth and released Catholics from their allegiance to
her—a step which put Edmund and men like him into
immediate danger. Now every Catholic was regarded as
a potential traitor.

During the following year he returned to England in
disguise and attended the trial in Westminster Hall of
John Storey, an elderly priest against whom Elizabeth
and her ministers had a special grudge. Kidnapped in
Antwerp, he was brought back to England and executed
with particular cruelty.

For Edmund events had pointed the way ahead:
within days he set sail for France and the priesthood. In
the English Channel his ship was stopped by a Government frigate. Edmund, who had no passport, was taken
off and brought back to Dover. Having parted with his
money and luggage, he was soon released. With the help
of a loan from friends he set sail once more and reached
Douai without further trouble. When news of his depar-
ture reached Cecil's ears, the Lord Treasurer expressed
his regret that so notable a man had left the country—"for
indeed he is one of the diamonds of England."

At the English College he was both pupil and professor: while mastering theology he taught rhetoric to fellow-students whose ages ranged from teens to sixties, several of his old Oxford friends among them. There is no evidence that at this time Edmund saw himself as a future martyr. He might very well have spent the rest of his life on the college staff, teaching and helping to produce the great Douai Bible.

During the next two years, however, the conviction grew within him that God intended him for something other than the life of scholarship which he loved so much and for which his talents so well fitted him. More and more, his thoughts turned to the Society of Jesus, whose fire and discipline would, he felt, make him what God wished him to be.

Travelling on foot to Rome, Edmund was received as a novice and sent to the Province of Bohemia, for although it already had a number of English members, the Society had as yet no separate province for them. At Brno, in what is now Czechoslovakia, the Oxford scholar performed the humble duties of farm and house and kitchen. His time there was the happiest of his life: afterwards he wrote with deep nostalgia of the dust and brooms and chaff, and of the companionship of his fellow-novices.

His studies for the priesthood, at Prague, were completed in five years. Ordained in 1578, he stayed on to teach. It looked as though Edmund was to live a scholar's life after all.

During the following year his old Rector at Douai, Dr. William Allen, asked for some Jesuits to be sent to England alongside the secular priests from his own college. In Germany, Poland and Bohemia the Society of Jesus had fought Protestantism with much success. Might it not do the same on the difficult and dangerous English mission?

One of the first priests to be chosen was Edmund
Campion. At last he saw clearly the vocation to which
God had called him. On the night before he left, a col-
league wrote in Latin over the door of his room: "Father
Edmund Campion, Martyr."

Travelling first to Rome, Edmund set out for England
in the Spring of 1580. There were fourteen in the party:
Jesuits, secular priests and two laymen. The senior was a
Bishop, Thomas Goldwell of St. Asaph. Now nearly
eighty, he had spent most of his life in safe Roman exile;
at Rheims his courage failed him and he turned back.

The journey was, however, not without its lighter moments. In his role as "Mr. Patrick," an uneducated servant, Edmund dared not admit to a knowledge of Latin.
When a curious stranger addressed him in that language,
he looked dumb and muttered: "Signor, No." The
stranger persisted: "Potesne loquere Latine?" The Latin
orator shrugged his shoulders and walked away.

At Geneva they were courteously received by Theodore Beza, the city's leading Calvinist theologian, who
said that he was sorry to hear that they were Catholics
but that he really did not have time to argue dogma with
them. Stung by this refusal, Robert Persons had to be
dissuaded from challenging the great man to a public
disputation, the loser to be burned alive in the market
place. Instead they had fun with a minister whom they
found placidly reading a sermon a mile out of town. After
Edmund and a colleague had tied him up in doctrinal
knots, he turned for support to their companions, only to
find himself in even worse trouble. They left him splut-
tering with indignation.

After singing a *Te Deum* on a hilltop in thanksgiving
for their jolly time in Geneva, the party crossed rough
ground to do penance at a local shrine. Consciences, it
seems, were pricking a little!

Though he joked often, as they all did, about the death
which awaited them, Edmund knew that he must pray
hard to be worthy of it. For hours, morning and night, he
would push on ahead of the rest, spending the time in
meditation and private devotion.

When they finally reached the Channel coast, they
split up and travelled from several different ports. A
group as large as theirs would immediately have attracted suspicion had they attempted to cross together.

In London he quickly discovered that many Catholics,
far from welcoming the Jesuits with open arms, greeted
their arrival with dismay. England's Protestant rulers
knew as well as anyone what the Society of Jesus had
achieved elsewhere. Now that its members were on English soil, would not official fear and hatred be vented on
the whole Catholic community? Worse still, what if the
Jesuits were actually to meddle in politics, in an effort to
restore a Catholic regime in England? Persecution, already severe, would certainly be redoubled.

To allay these fears Edmund and Robert swore an oath
that they had come for the good of souls and would not
undertake political action of any kind. Yet it was not this
assurance that swiftly won over the doubters, but the
Jesuits' courage and dedication, and the special skills
which they brought to their task. The situation in which
Catholics found themselves constantly produced new
and difficult cases of conscience with which priests
trained in the traditional mode were ill-equipped to
cope. The advice of the Jesuits, specialists in moral
theology, was eagerly sought by their suffering and bewildered fellow-countrymen.

Soon we find Edmund was writing to his Father General of the "exceeding reverence" with which they are
treated by priests and layfolk alike. More Jesuits are ur-
gently needed and, he emphasises, they must be the best

the Society can provide: men who will prove equal to all
that English Catholics expect of them.

In his letter Edmund paints a vivid picture of his life
on the run. The different disguises which he is forced to
adopt often make him feel ridiculous. His name, too, he
is constantly changing. Frequently he reads or is told, by
people who are quite sure of the fact, that Campion, the
notorious Jesuit, has been taken.

While authority thunders against him, brave Catholics
readily risk their own safety to give him shelter. All the
time, converts come into the Church, waverers are
strengthened and the lapsed are reconciled: "The har-
vest indeed is wonderful great. . . . ."

Yet never for a moment does he deceive himself. His
dashing, heroic style masks a sober realism: "I cannot
long escape the hands of the heretics. The enemy have so
many eyes, so many tongues, so many scouts and crafts."

Once he was captured, Edmund knew, he might have
little chance to explain why the Jesuits had come to England, or to counter the lie that they planned the over-
throw of the Government and the death of the Queen. So
he published the remarkable document known as
"Campion's Brag."

In our own day brave men have frequently proclaimed
their truth under the noses of tyrants, yet no *samizdat* has
quite equalled the panache of Edmund's challenge.
After a brief personal history, he affirms once more that
his mission is spiritual and not political. He then begs the
opportunity to argue his position with the best Anglican
theologians. Queen Elizabeth herself, he suggests, might
deign to honor some of these debates with her presence.
When his adversaries have listened to the Catholic case,
he is convinced, they will quickly see on what a sure
foundation the Church of Rome stands. His final words
are moving indeed:

Many innocent hands are lifted up to heaven for you daily
by those English students, whose posteritie shall never
die, which beyond seas, gathering virtue and sufficient
knowledge for the purpose, are determined never to give
you over, but either to win you to heaven, or to die upon
your pikes. And touching our Societie, be it known to you
that we have made a league—all the Jesuits in the world,
whose succession and multitude must overreach all the
practices of England—cheerfully to carry the cross you
shall lay upon us, and never to despair your recovery,
while we have a man left to enjoy your Tyburn, or to be
racked with your torments, or consumed with your prisons. The expense is reckoned, the enterprise is begun; it
is of God, it cannot be withstood. So the faith was planted:
so it must be restored. If these my offers be refused, and
my endeavours can take no place, and I, having run thousands of miles to do you good, shall be rewarded with
rigour, I have no more to say but to recommend your case
and mine to Almightie God, the Searcher of Hearts, who
send us His grace, and set us at accord before the day of
payment, to the end we may at last be friends in heaven,
when all injuries shall be forgotten.

He preached with particular success in Lancashire,
where the Catholic faith was—and still is—strong. Some
of his hearers remembered his sermons fifty years afterwards; after a century their children could still quote
from them. At this time he was writing the *Decem Rat-
iones*, a Latin treatise setting out ten reasons why he was
convinced that he could defeat the Protestants in argument. Printed in conditions of the utmost difficulty, it
caused a huge sensation when it appeared overnight on
the benches of the University Church in Oxford.

Furious at its success, the Government spurred the
priest-hunters to redouble their efforts. Edmund, already
England's most wanted man, made for Norfolk. His
enemies would not expect to find him there.

On the way he stayed at Lyford Grange in Berkshire, the home of the Yate family. Mr. Yate was in prison for his religion: the household consisted chiefly of his mother, some nuns to whom he had given protection, and two priests, Fathers Ford and Collington.

Edmund said Mass and departed quietly; only after he had left, did the Catholic neighbors discover the great Father Campion had been at the Grange. Tracked to an inn near Oxford, he was beseeched to turn back to Lyford, where many eager souls awaited him. So it was that on July 16, 1581, Edmund Campion once more said Mass at the Grange.

Among the congregation was one George Eliot, formerly a manservant in Catholic households, more recently, a prisoner held on charges of rape and homicide. Eliot had once worked with the Yate family's cook and it was through this old acquaintance that he had gained admission that Sunday morning. The cook knew nothing of Eliot's trouble with law: still less that he had obtained his release by offering to turn priest-catcher.

For an hour after Mass Eliot listened quietly to Edmund's sermon, his hand straying often to the Queen's commission in his pocket. The sermon-text was from the day's Gospel: "Jerusalem, Jerusalem, thou that killest the prophets." Never, it was recalled afterwards, had Edmund preached so fervently.

It was one o'clock when Eliot returned with the search-squad. Three times they ransacked the house, splintering panels whenever they found them hollow. Not until next morning, when they were almost ready to give up, did the searchers find the three priests, lying together in a secret chamber near the top of the house.

When they set out for London, the prisoners numbered four. Knowing nothing of the raid, Father William Filby had called at Lyford and walked into the soldiers' arms.

During the journey Edmund was pleasant and courteous to his captors and his charm quickly won them over. Eliot, the Judas, was ignored by all. Never once did those kind, unafraid eyes turn toward him.

"Mr. Campion, you look cheerfully upon everyone but me," he blurted out when he could bear it no longer. "I know that you are angry with me for this work."

"God forgive thee, Eliot, for so judging of me," Edmund replied. "I forgive thee, and in token of it, I drink to thee." Raising his cup, he added gravely, "If thou repent and come to confession, I will absolve thee. But large penance must thou have."

As the procession neared London, no doubt to the repugnance of all, the official humiliation began. The prisoners' arms were pinioned and upon the most prominent was hung a label: "This is Campion, the seditious Jesuit."

In the Tower Edmund was shut up in the notorious "Little Ease," a cell which may still be seen. There he was held for four days in a space so cramped that he could neither stand nor lie down.

Then the door was unlocked and within minutes Edmund found himself in a boat. Passing through Traitor's Gate, the oarsmen pulled hard upriver to Leicester House. There he was hustled through the ante-rooms into a chamber where, to his astonishment, he found himself staring into the hard eyes of the Queen.

He forced his cramped limbs to kneel. Elizabeth responded with a curt nod. At first her aides did the talking, then the monarch cut in impatiently. "Do you or do you not acknowledge me as Queen?" she demanded.

"Truly, Your Majesty, I do so acknowledge you in all temporal matters," replied Edmund.

The Government, he was told, had nothing against him but his Catholicism. "Which is my greatest glory," he replied mildly.

They offered him freedom and a prosperous future if

he would forswear Rome and resume his Anglican career. Edmund shook his head.

He had already promised that, "come rack, come rope," he would never betray his friends. Returned to the Tower, he was racked three times. He kept his word. Asked afterwards how he felt, he replied: "Not ill, because not at all."

Edmund had demanded a debate with leading Anglican theologians. Now he got it. Four times he was brought out to confront them; they lolling at their ease, he pain-ridden, ill and doomed. Refused either books or writing materials—with which they were well provided—he still trounced them thoroughly. Boldly he dared them to show him their copies of St. Augustine and St. John Chrysostom, so that he could prove his point. They could only respond by jeering when he made a slip of the tongue in Greek.

He showed the same spirit at his trial, attacking the prosecution witnesses vigorously. "What truth may you expect from their mouths?" he demanded. "One has confessed himself a murderer, the other a detestable atheist, a profane heathen, a destroyer of two men already. On your consciences would you believe them—they that have betrayed both God and man, nay, that have nothing left to swear by, neither religion nor honesty? Though you would believe them, can you?"

The charge of treason was plainly false, yet nothing that he said could affect the outcome of the trial; that he knew well enough. When the inevitable sentence was announced, he showed neither fear nor surprise. "If our religion do make us traitors," he told his judges, "we are worthy to be condemned. Otherwise we are, and have been, as good subjects as the Queen ever had."

To the condemned cell his sister was sent, to offer him, for the last time, freedom and prosperity if he would only return to the Anglican Church. Once again he refused.

He had, too, another visitor. George Eliot, loathed by everyone, had developed a paranoid fear that vengeful Catholics were out to kill him. Desperately he begged Edmund to believe that he had not realised that his act of betrayal would bring him to Tyburn. He had only expected him to receive a prison sentence.

Urging him once more to repent and confess his sins, Edmund assured him that he had nothing to fear from any English Catholic. However he was willing, if Eliot wished it, to recommend him to a Catholic duke in Germany, where he could feel perfectly safe. Edmund's generosity so moved one of his jailers that he afterwards became a Catholic.

Two other priests, Alexander Briant and Ralph Sherwin, accompanied Edmund Campion on the terrible journey to Tyburn. All three were dragged on hurdles through streets deep in mud. Sometimes people asked their blessing from the crowd. Once a gentleman stepped forward and wiped Edmund's face.

On the scaffold an Anglican minister tried to direct his prayers. Edmund, courteous as always, begged him to desist, since they were not of one faith. Protestant bystanders, not liking Latin, demanded that he pray in English. Edmund replied that he would "pray God in a language that they both well understood."

Still they goaded him: he should ask the Queen's forgiveness. Once more Edmund denied that he or his friends were traitors; he prayed for the Queen and wished her a long reign with all prosperity.

They were his last words. The cart was driven from under him, then the executioners cut him down. By that time he was mercifully unconscious, perhaps already dead.

10

Eleven Years in the Tower

As Edmund Campion's body was ripped
open and the entrails thrown into a cauldron, a spot of
blood splashed on to the coat of Henry Walpole, a young
man-about-town and a Catholic of sorts, who had posi-
tioned himself beneath the scaffold to get a good view.
From that moment Henry's life changed. He left England just as Edmund had done, entered the Society of
Jesus and in due course was ordained a priest. Thirteen
years after that fateful day at Tyburn, Henry himself died
the same death on the scaffold at York.

Henry Walpole was not the only man whom Edmund
converted during his last days on earth. When the Anglican theologians confronted him in the Tower of London's
chapel, they were evidently hoping to kill his intellectual reputation before they killed him. That was why
they employed tactics that were so grossly unfair. The
contest had, however, a result which Elizabeth and her
advisers never bargained for.

Among the watching courtiers stood another playboy,
Philip Howard, the popular young Earl of Arundel and

Surrey. As a teenager, Philip had seen his father Thomas,
Duke of Norfolk, beheaded in the Tower on a charge of
treason. Though himself a Protestant, the Duke had
plotted to marry the Catholic Mary, Queen of Scots. Why
he wished to do so is not at all clear; he was certainly sincere in his Protestantism and he insisted to the end that
he never intended to dethrone Elizabeth. Yet beheaded
he was.

"Beware of the court," Thomas Howard had warned
his son in a farewell letter. Philip, a clever young man,
ignored the warning and plunged himself into court life,
becoming a favorite of the queen who had executed his
father. Meanwhile he treated his young wife, Anne,
abominably. For a time they lived apart while Philip
pursued his amours among the ladies of the court.

Yet all the time he knew that the life which he led was
worthless. Once he actually talked things over with a
Catholic priest, but the meeting came to nothing. Now,
watching the doomed and tortured Edmund Campion
bravely defending his faith against his persecutors,
Philip knew that he, too, must become a Catholic.

It was no easy decision. For months a battle raged inside him. Like St. Augustine he wanted to be good, but
not yet. For a while he tried to bury his conscience in
games and parties, but they brought him no happiness.
Reconciled with Anne, he began to spend less and less
time at court. Soon a baby was on the way.

Angry at the loss of her favorite, the Queen had Anne
taken from her home and kept under house arrest while
the baby was born. Though Anne was a Catholic, Philip
named the little girl Elizabeth and had her baptized a
Protestant.

This was the last, despairing act of Philip the time-
serving courtier, the old Philip who was nearly dead.
Months later he was received into the Church. Life at

court, he realized, would be impossible. He wrote for
advice to William Allen, the former Douai Rector who
was now a Cardinal in Rome. The Government, inter-
cepting the letter, forged a reply which advised Philip to
flee the country.

It was a clever trick and Philip fell for it. By leaving
England without permission he was laying himself open
to a charge of contempt. Arrested at sea, he was brought
back to London. Like his father before him, Philip Howard became a prisoner in the Tower.

Deprived of the sacraments, he nevertheless spent
hours each day in prayer. Elizabeth would not let him
see his wife and daughter, and when Anne bore him a
long-awaited son and heir, the Queen had the news kept
from him.

For a time Philip was helped by letters sent in secretly
from one of Anne's friends, the Jesuit poet Robert
Southwell. Robert was himself to become a prisoner and
although he spent three years in the great fortress, he and
Philip never met. Eventually Robert made the journey to
the gallows at Tyburn, where feeling for him ran so high
among the crowd that, like Edmund Campion, he was
not cut down until he was almost certainly dead.

Tried and sentenced on the usual trumped-up evidence, Philip calmly awaited his own summons to
Tyburn or Tower Hill. It never came. Whether for fear of
public opinion, or because she wanted to play cat-and-
mouse, Elizabeth let him live in the Tower for nearly
eleven years.

Each day of his imprisonment, Philip grew weaker in
body but stronger in soul. He had always been especially
fond of the open air and during the early days of his
imprisonment he was allowed a daily walk around the
garden. Because he was so popular, people would gather
on Tower Hill to watch him. Soon his walk was forbidden

and he was confined to his cell. Philip made no complaint.

Over a fireplace in the Beauchamp Tower he carved a
Latin inscription which may still be read: *Quanto plus
afflictionis pro Christo in hoc saeculo tanto plus gloriae
cum Christo in futuro* (The more affliction for Christ in
this world, the more glory with Christ in the future).

During his long years of imprisonment Philip had two
companions, a faithful servant named Dix and a pet dog.
Once, during Robert Southwell's stay in the Tower, the
dog had found its way to the poet's cell. Philip said afterwards that he loved the dog all the more because it
had met his Jesuit friend.

A few months after Robert's execution, Philip was
taken suddenly ill at dinner. Realising that his end was
near, he begged once more to be allowed to see Anne
and the children. Elizabeth replied that she would grant
his request, and restore him to his former position as
well, if only he would abjure the Catholic religion. It was
a cruel answer, for the Queen must have known that she
was asking the impossible. Yet still there was no bitter-
ness: politely, Philip told the Lieutenant of the Tower
that he could not accept the condition.

This Lieutenant, Sir Michael Blount, had treated
Philip harshly throughout his imprisonment. Now, as
Philip lay dying, his jailer underwent a remarkable
change of heart. Kneeling beside his bedside, he asked
Philip to forgive him. This forgiveness the dying man
granted with the utmost kindness and sincerity.

To it, however, he added a plea and a warning. First,
he begged Sir Michael to be kinder to prisoners who
might come under his charge in the future. It was a hard
enough fate, Philip told him, to be shut up in the Tower;
for a jailer to add to a prisoner's afflictions was sheer

cruelty. "Your commission is only to keep with safety, not to kill with severity," he declared.

Then came the warning—one which Philip, who had once been the Queen's favorite, was well qualified to give. "Remember, Mr. Lieutenant," he said, "that God who with His finger turns the unstable wheel of this variable world, can in the revolution of a few days bring you to be a prisoner also, and to be kept in the same place where now you keep others. There is no calamity that men are subject unto, but you may taste as well as any other man."

When the Lieutenant left the cell he was weeping, though he little knew how quickly Philip's words would be realised. Seven weeks after his prisoner's death he fell into disgrace, lost his post, and was himself locked up in the Tower over which he had once ruled. His successor as Lieutenant, it is recorded, treated him as harshly as he had once treated others.

Philip Howard died peacefully at noon on Sunday, October 19, 1595. Though spared the axe and the rope, he stands with Edmund Campion and Robert Southwell among the forty English and Welsh martyrs who were canonised in 1970.

11

The Last Martyr

Early in the year 1670 a certain Captain Roberts, complete with sword, wig and pistols, set out by coach from London for the Welsh port of Holyhead. The gallant captain had recently travelled across Europe without experiencing any of the troubles which afflicted him on this, the last stage of his journey. Three times, sitting in the carriage, he and his fellow-passengers found themselves up to their knees in water, such was the state of the winter roads. When he finally got to Holyhead, adverse winds kept him waiting twelve days for a boat to Dublin.

On board at last, he spent much of the voyage standing by the rail, his eyes straining for a first glimpse of the Irish coast. After 25 years, Oliver Plunkett, Archbishop of Armagh and Primate of Ireland, was going home.

Oliver had been just a boy of sixteen when he set out for Rome to begin his studies for the priesthood. As a student at the Irish College, he swore an oath, as required by the college statutes, to return to his homeland as soon as he was ordained.

When that great day came, however, the young priest petitioned to be allowed to stay in Rome on the grounds that, Ireland being now in the grip of Oliver Cromwell, it was impossible to return there. This apparent timidity has troubled more than one of his biographers and some have striven to cover it with a cloak of decorum. These well-intentioned efforts are surely unnecessary. The truth is simply that Oliver, though already holy, was not yet holy enough for martyrdom.

He was certainly clever. With a string of degrees to his name—including doctorates in civil and canon law—he became a Professor at the Propaganda College, in whose chapel he had been ordained. He occupied, with great distinction, the Chairs of Theology and Controversy. In his leisure time he did nursing work in Rome's Santo Spirito Hospital, where he cheerfully performed the humblest and least congenial tasks.

In March, 1669, Edmund O'Reilly, Archbishop of Armagh, died an exile in France. Oliver, having heard the news, decided that at last it was time to go home.

Nothing in his colorful career is quite so strange as his appointment as Primate. Quite simply, he asked for the post and got it. His letter of application went like this:

> Most Eminent and Most Reverend Lords: Oliver Plunkett, most devoted petitioners of your Eminences, having read two courses of Speculative and Moral Theology for one year, and Controversies of the Christian Faith for three years, in the College of Propaganda Fide, and having served for many years as a consultor in the Sacred College of the Index, now desirous of returning to his native land for the service of souls, begs your Eminences to honor him with the Archbishopric of Armagh: petitioner being a native of the Armagh province. And he will pray God for your Eminences.

The document, which is still in existence, has raised even more eyebrows than his earlier request to remain in

Rome. Yet it was not written from motives of worldly ambition. Though Cromwell was now dead and Charles the Second on the throne, Ireland was still no safe place for a Catholic Bishop. Poor Archbishop O'Reilly had died on foreign soil and Oliver, when he did return, was forced to travel in disguise. At best, the Catholic religion was grudgingly tolerated by Ireland's Protestant overlords. Outbreaks of persecution were frequent and nobody knew when the next one would begin. Oliver's appointment might, indeed, provoke it; for the episcopal purple made the more bigoted Protestants see red.

In asking to be made Archbishop, therefore, Oliver was not looking forward to homage and fine robes but to hardship, poverty and danger. His letter is a sober and modest effort—almost offhand. He understates his academic qualifications and shows no real anxiety to be appointed. He would doubtless have been happy, had authority so decided, to continue his teaching and nursing in Rome. He applied for the See of Armagh because he believed that he was the best man for the job. And he was right.

About the sacrifice that might be demanded of him, he had no illusions. When he called at Santo Spirito to say good-bye, the hospital's saintly Polish Prior, Jan Mieskow, told him: "You are now going to shed your blood for the Catholic faith."

"I am unworthy of such a favor," Oliver replied, "nevertheless, it is my desire. Aid me with your prayers that it may be fulfilled."

For security reasons his episcopal ordination took place in Belgium. His next stop was London, where he stayed in St. James's Palace as the guest of Father Philip Howard, O.P., grandson of the martyr and chaplain to Charles's Portuguese Queen. So cold was the London winter that year, Oliver reported, that the wine froze in his chalice.

For the capital's persecuted Catholics, the climate was cold all the time: they had no Bishop and it is probable that Oliver confirmed many of them in secret. Later the Government imposed an oath on them which drew from Oliver a typically dry comment: "Among its beautiful clauses there is one which deserves to be remarked, that forsooth the Pope is a heretic."

Back home at last, the new Primate had a joyful reunion with the country's sole Bishop still living there in freedom. Patrick Plunkett, the elderly Bishop of Meath, was Oliver's kinsman. It was he who, as a Cistercian abbot, had given the youngster his early education and arranged for his studies in Rome.

Oliver's metropolitan province covered a third of Ireland. Its Catholic people, evicted from their homes and farms to make way for Protestant settlers, were desperately poor and so were the clergy who served them. Many priests had no home at all; others lived in hovels so small that their Archbishop had to crawl on hands and knees to enter the door. To keep themselves alive they usually had to keep cattle or cultivate the land.

Where the Protestant landowner would not allow a "Mass-house" to be built, Mass was said secretly in the open air. Because Catholic education was forbidden, children were taught the faith in secret "hedge-schools," often by priests who were themselves poorly educated.

Yet persecution, as so often before and since, only served to make the faith of the people stronger. "Better could not be found in the whole world," wrote Oliver, deeply moved. Few had been confirmed. Now that the opportunity had arrived, they travelled miles over moor and mountain, carrying the children, the aged and the sick on their backs. "They swarm to Confirmation like flies," Oliver reported.

That his clergy were poor did not distress Oliver unduly. "Wooden chalice, golden priest: golden chalice, wooden priest," he would say. When the Viceroy of Ireland commented on the poverty of Ireland's Catholic Bishops, the Primate replied spiritedly that they were happy to imitate the example of the early Church.

"Ah, but they are not like the Bishops of France and Spain," observed the Viceroy.

"My Lord, the Bishops of France and Spain would live poorly too, if the need arose," Oliver retorted.

Privately, though, he had reservations about the value of such extreme poverty, at least where Bishops were concerned. Without homes of their own, he and his colleagues were compelled to cadge meals from the Catholic gentry, of whom there were a few.

"They go today to the house of one gentleman and tomorrow to the house of another, not without their shame; and indeed the gentry are now tired of these visits," he told Rome ruefully. What was even worse, those who fed the Bishops often claimed the right to have their own favorites appointed to parishes, and the priest in question might not be the right man for the job.

Besides making it difficult to maintain episcopal dignity, or even authority, he added, the Bishops' beggary prevented them from meeting Protestants, most of whom were well-heeled. In this way valuable opportunities were lost.

Yet Oliver's own charm, learning and diplomacy soon triumphed over this adversity. Swiftly he established a rapport with the Viceroy and with other Establishment worthies. Lord Berkely, a liberal-minded man, had a Catholic wife, and sons at a Jesuit school in France. His lordship sportingly turned a blind eye when Oliver opened two schools in Drogheda—one of them for the education of priests—and put both into the charge of the Jesuits.

Raising clerical standards was among his most urgent tasks. In the difficult conditions of the time, ecclesiastical discipline had suffered badly. Priests, poorly trained and long cut off from authority, were frequently leading unsatisfactory lives. In particular, many had turned to the bottle as a relief from their woes.

In Rome Oliver had enjoyed a glass of wine. For a time, indeed, he had actually owned a small vineyard. Now, declaring himself a teetotaller, he forbade priests to frequent public houses or to drink whiskey. Of clerical tippling he declared: "Give me an Irish priest without this vice, and he is assuredly a saint." His own pledge he kept so thoroughly that he would not even take wine with his meals.

As a disciplinarian, Oliver was bound to make enemies and make them he did. Some of them, later, were to take terrible revenge.

For the moment, however, nothing caused more controversy than his dealings with the gangs variously known as *Rapparees* (robbers) or *Tories* (fugitives). Robbed of their homes by the Protestant settlers, they roamed Ireland's highways relieving Catholic and Protestant alike of money and goods. A few were Robin Hood figures who robbed the rich to help the poor; many more were criminals pure and simple.

In Ulster they were a serious scourge and Oliver resolved to meet them face to face. For an hour he preached to them, and it says much for his eloquence that at the end, fifteen of the twenty-one Rapparee leaders agreed to leave the country and go to France, aided by a safe-conduct and a £100 grant from the Government.

Some of Oliver's colleagues were unhappy at his role in the affair. It was not seemly, they felt, for a Primate to negotiate with highwaymen. Peter Talbot, Archbishop of Dublin, was most incensed. "Here he is now, with his fifteen bandits in tow, all arrived in the capital city of my diocese," he observed cuttingly.

The incident naturally raised Oliver's stock among fair-minded Protestants, who learned to respect him despite themselves. The Anglican Bishop of Derry, hearing him defend Catholicism, pronounced himself impressed. "As he is the first in dignity, so he is the first in learning among the Papists," he told his colleagues.

Oliver found a true and powerful friend in the Earl of Charlemont, Guardian of Ulster. "Have no fear, no-one dare touch you," he assured the Primate, "and when you want to administer Confirmation, don't go any more to the mountains. Come to the courtyard of my palace."

The Earl actually gave Oliver a house, together with two fields and an orchard, so making him the only Bishop in Ireland with a home of his own. To the orchard the Archbishop called children to receive religious instruction. It was his own hedge-school and a highly popular one, especially in the fall!

In Ireland officialdom might indeed smile on Oliver, graciously or grudgingly. But it was in London that power lay. In 1673 the "Merry Monarch" issued an anti-Catholic edict, with much regret, on the grounds that Parliament was about to do so anyway. A royal decree, King Charles argued, could be revoked at will, whereas an Act of Parliament, once on the statute-book, would be extremely difficult to remove. Therefore he was actually doing Catholics a good turn by legislating against them!

The royal benevolence prevented Oliver and his fellow-prelates from exercising their office and turned them into fugitives. With John Brennan, Bishop of Waterford, the Primate hid out in the mountains of South Armagh, where he wrote a vivid account of their hardships:

The hut in which Dr. Brennan and myself have taken
refuge is thatched with straw; when we lie down to rest,
we can see the stars through the roof; and when it rains
we are refreshed, even at the head of the bed, by each
successive shower. We find it difficult to procure even a
little oaten bread, yet we choose rather to die of hunger
than to abandon our flocks. . . . .

The hunt tightened and the pair were forced to take to
their heels in a blizzard. Snow and hail beat into their
eyes and often they were in danger of being buried in
deep drifts. Reaching a friendly house, they were hidden
for eight days in an unheated garret; Oliver was racked
with toothache and Bishop Brennan was suffering so
badly from rheumatism that he could not move his arm.
Oliver's health was damaged permanently by the ordeal
and his eyesight impaired.

After fifteen months the persecution died down. Oliver
and the rest could now come out of hiding. Still, though
there were severe restrictions, often these were applied,
or not applied, at the whim of some local official.

The comparative calm lasted for three years. Then, in
September, 1678, the good Protestants of Britain were
informed of a vast Jesuit conspiracy to assassinate
Charles the Second, put the Catholic Duke of York on the
throne, and reclaim England for the Catholic Church.

The "Popish Plot" was the invention of Titus Oates, an
Anglican clergyman and sometime student for the
Catholic priesthood. Having been expelled from sem-
inaries in France and Spain, Oates now traded on his
former connections to make people believe his wild
story. When the magistrate to whom he had made a
statement was found dead in mysterious circumstances,
many were ready to believe that the Papists had done
away with him.

In the wave of national hysteria which followed, Pro-

testant mobs roamed London cracking Catholic skulls.
Innocent people were arrested by the score; of these, no
fewer than thirty-five subsequently died on the scaffold.
Charles the Second, a weak king fighting for his throne,
signed the death-warrants with tears in his eyes.

Again, Catholic Bishops were banned from Ireland;
already Archbishop Talbot was in jail. Oliver, once more
in hiding, heard that Bishop Plunkett was dying in Dublin.

A few days later, a gentleman in a light-colored wig,
announced as "Mr. Meleady" appeared in the sick-room.
Oliver had come to bid his old tutor good-bye. A priest
who knew of the visit talked carelessly. On December 6,
1679, Oliver Plunkett was arrested.

The Earl of Shaftesbury, a notorious anti-Catholic
rabble-rouser, had determined to implicate Ireland in
the Popish Plot and Oliver was his chosen scapegoat. An
attempt was made in Dublin to try the Primate for
treason. It collapsed ludicrously when the principal
prosecution witnesses, two renegade priests with a
grudge against him, failed to appear.

The second trial, in London, was managed with more
finesse. The court refused Oliver the time he needed to
bring witnesses from Ireland, and this time the prosecution had no more than four ordained perjurers lined up to
swear his life away—though one of these, to his credit,
suffered last-minute pangs of conscience and tried to
withdraw.

During months in custody, Oliver's health had de-
teriorated badly: he now suffered from gallstones and he
looked, and felt, an old man. Though still in his early
fifties, he actually described himself as "very ancient and
subject to divers infirmities."

Ancient or not, he worked hard at his defence, even
though he was conducting his case under terrible handi-

caps. Himself a trained lawyer, he cross-examined the
mendacious witnesses with considerable skill. With icy
logic he poured scorn on the allegation that he had raised
and financed an army of 70,000 men, holding in readiness to support a French invasion of Ireland, and that he
had fixed upon Carlingford as the invaders' landing-
point. As he told the jury:

> A jury in Ireland consisting of men that lived in that coun-
> try, or any man in the world that hath seen Ireland in a
> map, would easily see there is no probability that that
> should be a place fit for the French to land in, though he
> never was in Ireland, yet by a map, he would see they
> must come between the narrow seas, all along to Ulster,
> and the rocks, and such places would make it very
> dangerous. . . . .

His eloquence was to no avail, as Oliver must have
realised from the beginning. Passing the inevitable sentence after the inevitable verdict, Chief Justice Pember-
ton brazenly exposed the real motive behind the trial.
"You have done as much as you could to dishonor our
God in this case," he roared, "*for the bottom of your
treason was your setting up your false religion, than
which there is not anything more displeasing to God, or
more pernicious to mankind in the world.*"

Oliver Plunkett was the last martyr to die for the
Catholic faith in England. Only the most crazed fanatics
really believed him guilty; King Charles himself, according to the French Ambassador, was distressed at the conviction of a man so obviously innocent. In his speech to
the crowd at Tyburn, on July 1, 1681, he forgave the
miserable wretches who had testified against him—men
who had resented the discipline which he had, as was his
duty, imposed upon them.

His Benedictine confessor, a fellow-prisoner in New-
gate, reported afterwards: "Many Protestants, in my

hearing, wished their souls in the same state with his. All believed him innocent; and he made Catholics, even the most timorous, in love with death."

Forty years later an old man called upon Archbishop Hugh McMahon, and haltingly admitted that he was Hugh Duffy, formerly a Franciscan priest and for many years afterwards a Rapparee bandit. Duffy was one of the four who had given false witness against Oliver at his trial. Now, in old age, his conscience tortured him.

"Is there to be no mercy for me?" he cried in anguish, throwing himself at the feet of the revolted prelate. In reply, Archbishop McMahon threw open the door of an oratory. To his horror, Duffy found himself looking into the dead face of Oliver Plunkett. The martyr's head, stricken from his body after the hanging, had been rescued from the executioner's fire and brought back to Ireland.

Poor Duffy fainted on the spot. When he recovered, he was reconciled to the Church. Oliver, we may be sure, helped him to make a good end.

12

An American Woman

Richard Bayley was a good doctor—too good not to realise what was happening to him. When the searing pain gripped his head and stomach, he knew at once that he had caught the yellow fever which was killing his poor Irish patients by the score.

When, after three days, no remedy had produced any improvement, he told the beautiful daughter at his side that he would not recover. "My Christ Jesus, have mercy on me!" he cried out repeatedly in his agony. On Monday, August 17, 1801, the pain eased. Soon afterwards, at 2:30 in the afternoon, Richard Bayley died.

"My Christ Jesus, have mercy on me!" In the days that followed, Elizabeth thought constantly of her father's dying prayer. Never before in all her twenty-seven years had she heard him even mention the name of Christ. Despite all his care for the poor, despite his formal membership of the Episcopalian Church, Dr. Bayley had brought his daughter up principally on Voltaire and Rousseau. Their rationalist spirit had been the driving-force of his life.

Elizabeth Ann Bayley was born in the then—
fashionable Battery district of New York on August 28,
1774. One of her descendants was to become Governor
of New York and then President of the United States—
Franklin Delano Roosevelt. Both her parents were of
English stock, though Richard also had some French
Hugenot blood which may have contributed the touch of
vivacity which his daughter so frequently displayed.

She was certainly a beautiful girl: petite, with finely-
cut features and a wealth of naturally-curled hair. But
she well knew her most attractive feature. "I imagine my
eyes were larger and blacker than usual," she wrote her
father after hearing one of his medical articles praised.
Those eyes were to go on working their magic to the end
of her days.

Among the many young men captivated by them was
William Seton, handsome son of a Scots merchant who
had settled in New York. "It is currently reported and
generally believed that I am to be married to Miss
Bayley, but I shall think twice before I commit myself in
any direction," he wrote, somewhat condescendingly.
However, he added, he admired her mental accomplishments and it would be a happy man who made
Elizabeth his wife.

Beautiful, intelligent, of good family, comfortably-off,
lacking no feminine accomplishment—it seemed as
though Elizabeth had everything. Her father, especially,
was devoted to her and she to him. In an age when young
ladies were generally expected to stick to music and
neddlework, he made her free of his bookshelves and
treated her as his equal. He even signed his letters;
"Your father and friend."

Yet at eighteen years of age, this apparently happy
young woman felt such a void at the heart of her life that

she actually entertained thoughts of self-destruction. She could see no purpose to existence. Then the crisis passed; the void was filled. In place of her father's well-bred deism, Elizabeth was given a warm and living relationship with Christ. At the age of twenty-six, she made her first Holy Communion in the Episcopal Church.

From childhood she had been naturally religious; now she became naturally Catholic. She read *The Imitation of Christ,* she wore a crucifix around her neck, she bowed her head at the name of Jesus, she was fascinated by the doctrine of the guardian angels—and she thought nuns' lives beautiful. Nobody taught her these things: the future founders of the Anglo-Catholic movement were yet in their English cradles. She had no Catholic friends and was subject to no Catholic influence save that of the Irish to whom her father ministered. Their faith and piety impressed her deeply as she watched them arrive, starving and disease-ridden, in the quarantine-camps of New York.

"The first thing these poor people did when they got to their tents was to assemble on the grass and all, kneeling, adored our Maker for the mercy; and every morning sun finds them repeating their praises," she wrote.

On January 25, 1794, cautious William Seton, having thought twice, took Elizabeth as his wife at Trinity Church in New York. William, immersed in his father's business, was at this time a conventional Christian, quite happy to leave Elizabeth to her Bible-reading and to her work for the poor.

When yellow fever swept through the Irish community, it was the plight of the young mothers and their babies which upset her most; for she was now a young mother herself. "Rebecca I can no longer sleep," she wrote her sister-in-law. "The dead and dying obsess my

mind. Babes perishing on the empty breasts of expiring
mothers. . . . . At this moment there are twelve children certainly doomed to die from mere want of food."

She planned to wean her own baby daughter early so
that she could give her breasts to one of the starving
infants; but her father, so soon to sacrifice his life, coun-
seled against it. Always an obedient daughter, Elizabeth
must nevertheless have exerted her own influence upon
Richard Bayley. Can anyone doubt that it was her example, coupled with her prayers, that led him to a Christian
end?

Her father's death was not the first of Elizabeth's mis-
fortunes. In 1798 the Seton family business had failed
and for the first time in her life Elizabeth experienced for
herself what it meant to be poor. True, her poverty was
not that of the starving Irish, but for someone of her
background it was bad enough. For a time she bore it
cheerfully, but in the end depression overtook her and
she sought spiritual direction at the hands of the Reverend Henry Hobart, Assistant Rector at Trinity
Church.

The next blow was more serious still. In 1803 William
Seton's health collapsed. The disease, apparently tuberculosis, attacked lungs and intestines. It was decided
that in Italy, where the Setons had friends, he would
have a better chance of recovery. On October 2, William
and Elizabeth set sail on board the brig Shepherdess. By
now there were five little Setons but only the eldest,
Anna, travelled with them.

Despite both storms and calms, the seven-week journey across the Atlantic was a happy one, thanks largely to
the kindness of the Irish sea-captain and his wife. It was
at Leghorn, where their voyage ended, that the nightmare began.

Because of the Italian fear of yellow fever, the Setons

were forced to spend a month's quarantine in a damp, unhealthy institution known as the Lazaretto. In this place, part hostel, part prison, poor William almost died.

Anna's courage and cheerfulness greatly cheered her parents during their ordeal. She loved to jump rope and Elizabeth, too, sometimes joined her in the exercise, chiefly to keep warm. Anna became a great favorite with the Italians, who called her "Annina." By this name she was known for the rest of her short life.

On December 19, the three were released from the Lazaretto, to be greeted at the gate by a sympathetic crowd. It must have been obvious to all that William had not long to live.

On a Christmas Day which passed without his wife's taking a mouthful of food, the dying man suddenly said: "How I wish we could have the Sacrament."

"Well, we must do all we can," replied Elizabeth.

They were in a small hotel at Pisa, far from any Anglican minister or church. Putting a little wine into a glass, Elizabeth read portions of the psalms and said some prayers of her own. Then they drank the wine together.

The pair arranged a signal between them, which William should give if, at the last, he were unable to speak. And give it he did.

"At a quarter past seven on Tuesday morning, December 27," wrote Elizabeth in her journal, "my poor husband gave his last sigh, with the strong pressure of the hand which he had agreed to give me at this moment if his soul continued in its peace with our Jesus."

William was buried next day in the Protestant cemetery at Leghorn, where the pale, beautiful young widow once more attracted much sympathy among the Italians. "If she were not a heretic, she would be a saint," murmured one.

During their imprisonment in the Lazaretto, the Setons

had received much kindness from the Filicchi family, rich Leghorn bankers who lived in a hundred-roomed palace and who had long been business associates of William's father. During the months that followed, they sheltered Elizabeth in their home and showed her every possible kindness, nursing her through a serious fever and supporting her financially.

"The sumptuous and splendid worship of Italy will not, I am sure, withdraw your affections from the simple but affecting worship of Trinity Church." So the Reverend Henry Hobart had written before she left the United States. But the Filicchis were devout Catholics and Elizabeth found herself, under their kind influence, studying their religion and sharing their worship. "This is what they call their Real Presence," an English sightseer murmured to her one day at the Consecration. Elizabeth, revolted at the brutal scepticism of the remark, realised how close to the Catholic faith she had come.

It was as a Protestant, however, that she returned to America, escorted by Antonio Filicchi, a happily-married man who nevertheless appears to have fallen in love with her. It was a totally selfless love, though, for Antonio had done as much as anyone to guide Elizabeth toward the Church. It was his wife, Amabilia, who trustingly insisted that he accompany her.

Home at last, Elizabeth was joyfully re-united with her four smaller children, who had been distributed among friends and relatives. She was also reunited with the Reverend Mr. Hobart.

On the journey over, Annina had more than once demanded anxiously: "Ma, are there no Catholics in America? Ma, won't we go to the Catholic church when we get home?" The second of these questions was, of course, the crucial one.

While Annina pleaded to be taught the "Hail Mary," Elizabeth found herself the rope in a tug-of-war between Henry Hobart and Antonio Filicchi. The one plied her with anti-Catholic tracts and arguments; the other, with equal fervor, pressed the claims of Holy Mother Church.

Conversion to Rome, as Elizabeth fully realised, would entail great worldly risks. A widow with five young children, vulnerable and without means, she would be cutting herself off totally from family and friends. Hobart, meanwhile, pressed his case with ever-mounting vigor. Unknown to Elizabeth, he was himself secretly drawn to the Catholic Church and was perhaps even then fighting off the temptation to enter its fold. He fought successfully, and died an Episcopalian Bishop.

In addition to her religious dilemma, her life was still overshadowed by the loss of her husband, though she steadfastly refused to sigh over him. "I play the piano in the evening for my children," she wrote Amabilia, "and after they have danced themselves tired, we gather round the fire, and I go over with them the scenes of David, Daniel, Judith, or other great characters of the Bible, until we entirely forget the present."

The little ones, whom she loved so dearly, were used by Hobart and others as one more argument against her threatened conversion. Dare she be responsible, they demanded, for taking William's children out of the church in which he had died such a holy death?

It was a wounding argument, and perhaps it accounts, at least, partly, for her long hesitation in taking the final step. And yet, it seems, her mind was already made up; for of this effort to deter her, she wrote:

I am a mother, and must answer for my children at the judgement seat, whatever faith I lead them to. That being

so, I will go peaceably and firmly to the Catholic Church.
For if faith is so important to our salvation, I will seek it
where true faith first began. . . . . The controversies on
it I am quite incapable of deciding, and as the strictest
Protestant allows salvation to a good Catholic, to the
Catholics will I go, and try to be a good one.

On March 15, 1805, to the Catholics she went. In Old
St. Peter's Church, Barclay Street, New York, Elizabeth
Bayley Seton was received into the Church, with Antonio Filicchi as her sponsor. She departed, she reported
afterwards, "light of heart and with a clearer head than I
have had these many long months."

Though she had now become a social outcast, her
sisters-in-law, Cecilia and Harriet Seton, made it plain
that her conversion would in no way lessen their affection
for her. To these two, and to their lately-dead sister, Rebecca, Elizabeth had always been especially close. A
few other Protestant friends, it must be added, loyally
and bravely stood by her.

At this time she was living in a state of genteel poverty
which she described, with her usual good humor, in a
letter to a friend:

If you could imagine the occupation of mending and turning old things to the best account, added to teaching the
little ones and having them always at my elbow, you
would believe me that it is easier to pray than to write.
Also I clean my own room, wash all the small clothes, and
have much more employment in my present situation
than ever.

For a year or more she earned a precarious living as a
schoolmistress, though the first school to employ her
closed after rumors flew round New York that the pro-
prietors were Catholics—which they were not—and that
the school had been opened in order to seduce Protestant
children to the Catholic faith

A fresh storm broke over Elizabeth's head when
Cecilia Seton, having recovered from a serious illness,
announced her intention of following her sister-in-law
into the Catholic Church. Her family employed various
forms of blackmail to dissuade her, including the threat
of deportation to the West Indies. Cecilia remained
adamant and was duly received. Elizabeth was, needless
to say, accused of luring her into Rome's clutches.

In the much smaller New York of those days, her own
conversion attracted a degree of attention which it is hard
for us to imagine today. It may, indeed, have helped to
provoke a riot in which Protestant families tried to burn
down that same Old St. Peter's Church where she had
been received. A Catholic parishioner was killed in the
melée.

To add to her distress, Elizabeth found that her children were being taunted on account of their new faith—
in which they were, nevertheless, extremely happy.
Young William clamored lustily to become one of the
"little priests"—his name for the altar boys.

It became plain that for the children's sake, if for no
other, she must leave New York. The chance came when
Father William du Bourg, President of St. Mary's Seminary, Baltimore, met her by chance in Old St. Peter's
parish-house. He wanted to start a Catholic school in
Baltimore. Would Mrs. Seton come?

The little house in Paca Street where Elizabeth lived
and ran the school, was the birthplace both of the American Sisters of Charity and of the parish-school system in
the United States. In the fall of 1808 a young Philadelphia girl named Cecilia O'Conway, who felt a strong
vocation to become a nun, was told of the wonderful Mrs.
Seton who taught school in Baltimore and was plainly
moving in the same direction.

Cecilia became Elizabeth's first postulant. Three oth-

ers soon followed and on the Feast of Corpus Christi,
1809, the five Sisters appeared for the first time in public
at Mass in St. Mary's Chapel. At this time they called
themselves Sisters of St. Joseph and wore a habit based
on the Italian widow's costume which Elizabeth had
worn since William's death: black dress and short cape,
with a small white muslin cap held on by a black band
and fastened under the chin.

Soon another Cecilia arrived. Despite her poor health,
Elizabeth's sister-in-law was determined to join the new
Order. Then came Harriet Seton, still a Protestant and
engaged to Elizabeth's half-brother, Dr. Barclay Bayley,
in New York. Harriet suffered agonies of indecision before finally becoming a Catholic, though not a nun; for
she died only five months later, still wearing her fiance's
locket. Four months after Harriet's death, Cecilia followed her.

Both her ailing sisters-in-law accompanied Elizabeth
and a nun companion on the journey to Emmitsburg in
Maryland, where a benefactor had given them land for a
mother house. So did Annina, who was later to die as a
postulant. The fifty-mile trip by covered wagon took several days. To Elizabeth's amusement dogs, pigs and
geese joined their human owners in coming out to stare
at these strange travellers.

At Emmitsburg, despite her own failing health,
Elizabeth kept the Rule with the utmost strictness, rising
at 4 a.m. and kneeling upright through the long hours of
prayer. Always solicitous for others, she was hard on herself, eating little and working much. The first winter in
their new home was a terrible one, for their shack had no
windows and the snow blew in. They had not enough
money for food, nor material for clothes. Small wonder
that health was so often poor and lives short!

Yet Elizabeth and her companions bore it all with un-
failing cheerfulness. Steadily her influence spread;

steadily her Order grew. Racked by tuberculosis, she kept all her beauty: a parent who placed his daughters in her care declared that he would willingly have made the 600-mile journey just to look into her eyes, even though she were not to speak a word. Since he was a lapsed Catholic she spoke a good many words, with the result that he soon returned to the Church.

It was at Emmitsburg that the Order became Sisters of Charity, with a Rule adapted from that drawn up by St. Vincent de Paul. Changes, however, were made. The original French Rule, in particular, decreed that widows who entered the convent must first entrust their children to others. This Elizabeth refused to do.

Of the remaining children Rebecca, like her elder sister, joined her mother's Order but died soon after taking her vows. Catherine became a schoolteacher and then, surprisingly enough, a Sister of Mercy. She lived to be 91. Richard, whom his mother called her "giant," tried banking with the Filicchis, found it was not for him, and died a heroic death at the age of 26. During a sea-voyage he nursed a priest who had fallen ill from an infectious disease, caught it himself, and succumbed. William also had an unsuccessful spell with the Filicchis before finding his career as an officer in the U.S. Navy.

Despite the cheerfulness and good sense which she radiated, and the confidence which she gave to others, Elizabeth did not always remain untroubled in spirit. We know that at least once, perhaps twice, she was tempted to abandon the Order which she had founded and flee to some new life elsewhere.

Yet she persevered and died happily, surrounded by her Sisters, on January 4, 1821. She was forty-six years old. Today the Order which she founded continues its great work all over the United States, and Elizabeth is America's first and only native-born saint.

13

The Little One

Nobody gave a second glance to the slightly-built man in the dark, clerical clothes as he walked Vine Street, Philadelphia, on a January afternoon in 1860. His appearance did not compel attention, nor did his manner invite it. The high-cheekboned face, kindly and serene, clearly showed his Slavic origins. He seemed pensive, as though his attention, in its turn, was fixed on something far beyond Vine Street's sights and sounds.

Near the junction with Thirteenth Street his steps faltered. The passers-by noticed him now, for he suddenly staggered and, a moment later, fell to the ground. Two men rushed forward and carried the frail load into the nearest house, 1218 Vine Street. Within minutes, surrounded by strangers, he died.

Only when they opened his overcoat and saw the pectoral cross did they guess his identity. John Neumann, Bishop of Philadelphia, had gone to his reward.

Typically, his last journey had been an errand for one of his priests—a humble errand, which he might easily have entrusted to a subordinate. A pastor in an outlying town had sent him a chalice to be consecrated. Bishop Neumann had not received it, so he set out himself to check at the express office. He never arrived.

John Neumann, most recently canonised of America's saints, was not yet forty-nine when death came to him. The son of a stocking-maker, he was born in the village of Prachatitz, in what is now Czechoslovakia, on March 28, 1811.

It was during his seminary days at Prague that John formed the ambition to go as a missionary to America. His studies completed, he hit his first major setback. Since there was no shortage of priests in the Prague area, no students from his class were to be ordained that year.

It was as plain Mr. Neumann, then, that John arrived in the United States on board the three-masted *Europa* in June, 1836. To be strictly accurate, the *Europa* brought him within sight of the United States: off Staten Island the captain announced that sick passengers must be cared for before the ship could proceed to New York, otherwise quarantine officials might send them back to Le Havre. Six times John asked to be allowed ashore: six times Captain Drummond refused. Persistence won in the end, however, and after three days of waiting, young John Neumann set foot in the land where he was to spend the rest of his life. It was the Feast of Corpus Christi.

"But why this fear, as if there were no God?" John had written in his diary before setting out from home. Every missionary needs more than the normal ration of courage, and John needed more than most. Alone and unknown, without a soul to greet him, he stepped ashore with only a dollar in his pocket. His shoes were worn and his clothes shabby; his hat had been stolen on the voyage.

His baggage contained a few spiritual books and little else.

Worst of all was the uncertainty about his future. In Europe he had tried to obtain an American post, without any apparent success. In those days transatlantic mail was slow and uncertain; he had used up his money waiting around in Paris for a reply to his application. He did not know for sure, now that he was in the States, that he would find a Bishop willing to ordain him.

His first night was spent in an inn. Next morning, with the inn keeper's help, he found a Catholic church where he could thank God for his safe arrival. From there the pastor directed him to St. Patrick's Cathedral, in those days situated on Mott Street.

Face to face with New York's seventy-eight-year-old Bishop, John Dubois, all John's misgivings about his future were immediately dispelled. Not only did Bishop Dubois welcome him: he told John that he had been awaiting him eagerly for weeks. His reply to John's letter had been sent immediately, but when it arrived the young hopeful was already on the high seas.

John received the three major Orders within a week: he was ordained priest on June 25, 1836. His first Mass, next day, was offered at St. Nicholas's Church, Second Street. New York's Catholic paper gave two lines to the new priest, spelling his name wrong in the process.

Bishop Dubois, a refugee from the French Revolution, ruled over a diocese which then included the whole of New York State and part of New Jersey. When John arrived, there were 200,000 Catholics, most of them Irish or German, with more arriving on every boat.

John must indeed have seemed a godsend: he knew eight languages, including English, and his German was fluent. For his first assignment he was sent to the Buffalo

area—a long journey accomplished mostly by canal-boat.
During a stopover at Rochester, he spent some time with
a Redemptorist, Father Prost. Though he did not realise
it at the time, the meeting was to influence his future life
profoundly.

John's first parish, at Williamsville, was 900 miles
square. As he rode out on his rounds, the young pastor
could hear the rushing of Niagara Falls. His 400 Catholic
families were mostly German and, like himself, new-
comers to the United States. The hardships were many:
miles of rough underbrush had to be cleared before the
land could be cultivated. Mosquitos plagued them in
summer and the winters were harsh in the extreme.
Often the farmers lacked money and even food. As for
their homes, let John himself describe them:

> They live in miserable shanties, some of which do not
> have even the luxury of a window. Chairs and bedsteads
> are, generally speaking, unknown. I have seen dying
> people stretched out on a heap of straw or moss. I have to
> sit beside them on the ground to hear their confessions
> and to prepare them for the Sacraments.

His church was unfinished—four stone walls with
neither flooring nor roof. The first time John said Mass
there, vandals threw stones over the walls, one landing
on the temporary altar.

Despite everything, he was radiantly happy: happy to
be in America, happy to be a priest at last, and one with a
flock of his own. He lived as poorly as the poorest of
them: sometimes they wondered if he got enough to eat.
They did not know that he had taken a private vow of
poverty. With his lifelong horror of material wealth, John
feared that handling parish funds might make him
greedy, so he resolved to live only on the necessities of
life.

Small wonder that his flock loved him, especially the children, for whom he often carried candy in his pockets. He taught them, not only doctrine, but the three R's as well.

Eagerly he planned ways of attracting other young priests to America. A mission-house in his native Bohemia and a German-speaking seminary in Buffalo were two ideas which never came to fruition. "You still sigh, if I am to believe you, for America and for your old friend," he wrote a seminary classmate. "Why, then, don't you come?" The friend did not come, nor did anyone else.

Standing only five-feet-four in his socks, John was often called "the little priest." His lack of inches, coupled with his diffident manner, made many think him a man who would easily be pushed around. They quickly discovered that they were wrong. Challenged to a public debate by the leader of a Protestant sect, he accepted reluctantly—and soundly defeated his opponent. When, on another occasion, a fanatic tried to argue with him, John walked away in silence. "Turn around and talk to me or I'll shoot you!" the man yelled, drawing a gun. John kept on walking. The man did not shoot.

In that vast territory a horse was an essential mode of transport. John was sorely lacking in equestrian talent. His chosen mount was a perverse and stubborn creature which took great delight in stopping dead and refusing to go further—often in the most inconvenient places. In other ways, too, it made life difficult for its young rider. Once it reached out and ate some rare flowers which John had just plucked from the roadside, and which he had been planning to send to botanist friends in Bohemia. "That was the sacrifice God wanted from me at that moment," he would say afterwards, laughing.

In September, 1839, John's younger brother, Wences-

laus, came out from home to join him. Though a layman,
Wenceslaus soon became invaluable as cook, house-
keeper, teacher, builder and general mission factotum.
He was a breath of home and also a big consolation for his
brother's disappointed hopes of drawing other priests to
America.

Despite the companionship of Wenceslaus, by now
John was no longer happy. The honeymoon period of his
priesthood was over; self-doubt and spiritual dryness
began to torment him. He felt himself beset by failure
and he thought of abandoning his flock for a hidden life
of prayer and penance.

Ill-health, brought on by overwork, may well have
been responsible for his ordeal. At all events, in 1840, he
suffered a breakdown. During his convalescence he con-
fided to his confessor a desire which he had felt for some
time. He wished to become a Redemptorist.

Since his first meeting with Father Prost, whose personality had so much impressed him, John had revisited
Rochester and seen for himself the increase in piety
which the Redemptorist had brought about among the
German population there. He felt drawn to life in a religious community and it was natural that he should
choose a Congregation whose members, in response to
the wish of their founder, St. Alphonsus Liguori, had
thrown themselves heart and soul into the American mission.

Life with the Redemptorists, he quickly discovered,
brought its own problems and trials. Reporting to the
Congregation's headquarters in Pittsburgh, he found that
he was to be his own novice-master and that he had to act
as parish priest in the bargain! From the few hard-
worked, much-travelling priests there, none could be
spared to give him the year of spiritual direction to
which he had been looking forward so eagerly.

"I daily made two meditations and two examens of conscience with the community," he recalled later, "spiritual reading in private, and a visit to the Blessed Sacrament. I recited the Rosary, also, and that was all."

Wenceslaus followed him into the Redemptorist Congregation as a lay-brother, which obviously brought John great joy. Yet soon he himself was once again racked by doubts as to whether he had done right in becoming a religious. These were not helped by a senior confrere who told him: "You had better go back to your old mission. You'll never be able to persevere with us!" No doubt the idea was to test his determination.

No doubt, also, John was writing from experience when he later analysed the temptations which beset the newcomer to the religious life:

This novice imagines himself deficient in physical strength, another deludes himself with the notion that things would go more smoothly in another Order, or that he could possibly do more for the honor of God while living in the world. Sadness and melancholy seize upon some while others are beset by a love of their own ease. Some are attacked by homesickness, or other temptations born of self-will, disgust for prayer, want of confidence in their superiors, and so forth. The temptations of the soul are doubtless as numerous as the disorders of the body, but to remain steadfast and to persevere in all this turmoil of spirit, there is no better remedy than prayer to the Blessed Virgin for the grace of perseverance. . . .

While undergoing his own private agonies, John was asked to conduct a mission at Randolph, Ohio, where hostility between two Catholic factions had become so bitter that one had burned down the church. The mission succeeded: peace returned to Randolph. But it was only after another breakdown that John found his own peace.

On January 16, 1842, he was professed as a Redemptorist.

In Pittsburgh and in Baltimore he worked devotedly as a pastor and his qualities soon drew the attention of the Congregation's highest superiors. He tackled business and financial problems, for which he had an acute distaste, with vigor and determination. When a notorious double murderer was publicly hanged in Baltimore, John was at his side on the scaffold. His presence made a deep impression on the crowd.

At this time the Redemptorists in the United States were controlled by the Belgian provincial, Father Louis De Held. His vice-regent in America, Father Peter Czackert, did not always see eye-to-eye with Father De Held. In December, 1846, after a particularly sharp disagreement, the provincial decided that Father Czackert must be replaced. Only three years after his profession, John Neumann found himself femporary superior of the entire Redemptorist mission.

"Father Neumann has only half the necessary qualities of a good superior, namely exemplary conduct and regularity. He lacks the all-important quality in America of force or authority. He never had this and he never will." Thus Father Ignatius Stelzig, one of the two priests appointed to assist John as consultor. Father Stelzig was a brilliant man, but he was also very young. He can surely be forgiven for making a mistake which others, far older and more experienced than he, had made in the past and were to repeat again and again in the future.

Among those misled by John's quiet and modest manner was the porter at the Redemptorists' New York house. This youngster, who had never met him, took him for a sacristan and asked him to sit on a bench until the pastor could see him. When the pastor appeared and knelt for the "sacristan's" blessing, the young porter was covered in confusion. John, unoffended and much amused, quickly put him at his ease.

"Although, as we shall see, he could be tough when the occasion demanded, he preferred tact and good humor in dealing with others' faults. In the parish school at Baltimore, a nun who was short on patience would suddenly find him beside her. "He used to enter the room so quietly and so modestly," she recalled, "that I did not notice him until he greeted me with the words: 'Sister, I thought I heard you screaming just now.' Then he would fix his large, expressive eyes on me so earnestly that there was no mistaking the meaning."

In the morning John would be the first among his colleagues to rise and they would come down to find him on his knees lighting the fire. At night, when they went to bed, he would be once more on his knees—in prayer.

During his tenure of office he opened new foundations in Detroit and in New Orleans—so fulfilling a prophecy made by St. Alphonsus long before. Walking with his students beside the Bay of Naples, the founder had noticed a ship marked "For New Orleans." He told the youngsters: "One day my sons will have a house there."

When Baltimore's Archbishop Eccleston wanted to dissolve the Oblate Sisters of Providence, a colored community whose numbers had dwindled to three, John intervened and took over the Order's direction. Soon their numbers multiplied—and they flourish to this day. Later John founded an Order of his own, a community of Franciscan tertiaries.

His toughness showed when lay trustees of Detroit's Redemptorist church refused to allow the Congregation to run parish affairs as they thought best. The Redemptorists took the case to court and eventually won.

This victory struck a powerful blow against the whole
system of lay trusteeism, which had caused much trouble
during the Church's early years in America.

On February 10, 1848, John became an American citizen. At the end of the year, by his own wish, he laid
down the burden of office. Despite all that he had
achieved—and I have been able to mention only a small
part—some of his confreres still found fault with him as
an administrator. "Do not be sorry for me," he told
well-wishers. "I have never done anything to become a
Superior and I will do nothing to remain one."

The two years that followed were comparatively
peaceful, though not idle, for John had made it a cardinal
rule never to waste a single minute of his life. He
preached, he wrote, he did pastoral work—and he became confessor to Baltimore's Archbishop Francis Kenrick, who had come to the diocese after twenty years as
Bishop of Philadelphia.

Obviously someone would have to be appointed to
Philadelphia in Archbishop Kenrick's place. There was
no doubt in the Archbishop's mind who that someone
should be. He told John that he would be recommending
his name to Rome.

John begged to be left out of the list of candidates, but
when the customary three names went to the Vatican, his
was among them. Asked for their opinion, the American
hierarchy were sharply divided. Some wanted John because he was holy, zealous, learned and could speak
German; others objected that he was quiet, that he
lacked personality, that he did not preach well and that
his English was less than perfect.

On a bright March day in 1852, Archbishop Kenrick
called at St. Alphonsus's Rectory in Baltimore. As it happened, John was out. When he returned, the Archbishop

had gone. On a table in his room lay an episcopal ring and a pectoral cross.

"God knows whom to choose and his choice is always the best," commented New York's Archbishop John Hughes when he heard that John Neumann was to be Bishop of Philadelphia. "I would rather die than be consecrated tomorrow," John told a friend on the eve of the ceremony. In far-off Prachatitz, his 80-year-old father at first refused to believe the news.

Along with his cope and mitre, John took on a huge load of debt and administrative work. Yet he rarely, if ever, refused to see anyone who called on him. He constantly gave money to the poor and he even gave them his clothes. When one of his priests told him that he looked shabby and should go and change into something neater, the Bishop replied quietly that he had nothing into which he could change.

He loved to travel around the diocese, and especially to the poorer and remoter areas, where he could say Mass and hear confessions in the kind of surroundings which he had known as a young priest. He seemed to return to his desk and its problems refreshed by these visits.

One of his very first episcopal acts was to set up a Central Board of Education, with both clerical and lay members, to build much-needed schools as soon as possible. Dioceses all over the United States later followed his example, and for this reason John is often called the "Father" of America's parish-school system. He certainly fathered its modern form.

He established an Italian parish in Philadelphia and so set up another "first." Most of his immigrant flock, however, were Irish or German. Inevitably there was rivalry, and even hostility, between the two factions. On one occasion some German hotheads, feeling that the Irish

were receiving undue favor, complained loudly that
their German Bishop was deserting the national cause.
"Thank God I'm not a German, I'm a Bohemian," John
told them coolly. In the circumstances, it was perhaps
not the most tactful of replies.

Enraged because he would not meet their demands,
some of the protesters put a railroad tie across the tracks
along which John was shortly to travel. Happily, it was
discovered in time.

Faced with yet another storm of abuse and recrimina-
tion, John listened in silence. When they had finished, he
replied simply: "I excommunicate you." The shocked
Germans soon repented and were soon received back
into the fold.

Despite the advice of his more cautious clergy, who
feared sacrilege by anti-Catholic fanatics, John established the Forty Hours devotion in the Philadelphia diocese. Here again he was setting a lead for others. He
worried much about this decision, but went ahead after
he seemed to hear a voice tell him that all would be well.

If John did indeed hear a voice, it was for him a rare
and probably unique experience. There are no miracles,
no visions in the life-story of John Neumann: just years of
hard and unrelenting work joyfully done for the Lord.
Sometimes there were consolations, though not often. In
1854 Pope Pius the Ninth invited him to Rome for the
formal proclamation of the Dogma of the Immaculate
Conception. Before returning to the United States, he
was able to visit his home in Bohemia where, despite his
hatred of fuss, he was given a gala welcome. After days
spent with his family, he left quietly, in the early morning. Tears ran down his face as he looked back at the
village for the last time.

When he became a Bishop, John took as his motto *Soli
Deo*—"For God Alone." Always hard on himself, he

drove himself harder still in order to fulfil it. He took even less sleep, would often miss breakfast, scourged himself with a discipline and wore a girdle of iron wire which penetrated his flesh. Though nobody knew of these mortifications, everyone knew that here was a Bishop of outstanding holiness. Even the Bishop of Pittsburgh, one of those who thought him timid and ineffectual, described John as "a man conspicuous for zeal and sanctity." A Benedictine Abbot, who knew him well, came nearer the mark. "I have always regarded him," he said, "as a little saint."

Since few bishops can have accomplished more in three short years, we can only assume that prejudice must have blinded John's critics to his achievements. Their opinion, in any case, troubled John not at all: in fact he agreed with them. In 1855 he asked Rome to transfer him to an easier diocese. "Because of my poor talents and lack of insight, I commit mistakes especially in the administration of temporal matters, and I fear these will involve me and my successors in greater difficulties and obligations," he wrote.

Instead of transferring him, Rome appointed a co-adjutor Bishop. James Frederick Wood, a convert, was as unlike John Neumann as any man could be. A tall, sophisticated extrovert, he had a strong "presence" and mixed easily with the upper classes, in whose company John was often uncomfortable. Years in the banking business had qualified him to handle financial affairs.

With Bishop Wood's help, John saw a roof placed on the cathedral building. Though he knew that the inside would not be finished for several years, he felt that an important milestone had been reached. Now he could look forward with greater confidence to the future.

Four months later a Redemptorist friend called to see him after lunch. The priest observed that John did not look well. John agreed that he felt strange, but thought that a walk in the fresh air would do him good. Before taking leave of the priest, John made a remark which was so unexpected as to be startling. "A man must always be ready," he said, "for death comes when and where God wills it."

A few minutes afterwards he set out on his last errand.

14

Go West. . . .

It was a nightmare crossing. For most of the passengers this was their first voyage and they were seasick from the moment when the ship's engines began to throb. Four days out of Le Havre, a storm blew up, spreading terror through the *Bourgogne* as she rolled and pitched her way through the fierce Atlantic waves. They arrived at last to find New York hidden under a blanket of fog. No skyline, no Statue of Liberty, to give them a compensatory thrill.

One of the most disappointed was a gentle-faced Italian nun who, with six sisters behind her, picked her way down the gangway towards the customs and immigration sheds. Though she had never planned to come to the United States, she had been looking forward to that famous first sight from the ship's rail.

A priest stepped forward, a young colleague at his elbow.

"Mother Cabrini?"

"Yes."

"I'm Father Morelli, Pastor of St. Joachim's. Bishop Scalabrini asked me to meet you."

In the rectory, after a good Italian dinner, the seven
nuns began to feel more cheerful. Their hosts belonged
to the Congregation of St. Charles Borromeo, founded in
Italy a few years before to work among Italian immigrants. Their founder, Bishop Scalabrini, had been one of
those responsible for the Sisters' coming to New York.
Supported by no fewer than three Cardinals, he had
urged that America, rather than China, was where their
work lay: America, where thousands of their fellow-
countrymen desperately needed the care which only
Italian-speaking nuns could provide. Pope Leo XIII had
clinched the matter with magisterial brevity. "Go not to
the East, but to the West," he commanded.

Now they were here and eager to begin work, seven
Missionary Sisters of the Sacred Heart. Dinner over, they
prepared to depart.

"Maybe you could show us the way to our convent?"
Mother Cabrini suggested.

Father Morelli looked at the floor, obviously embarrassed. "Mother," he replied, "I'm afraid you don't have
a convent."

The sisters looked at him, dumbfounded. What could
he be saying? When they left Italy, all had been arranged. Archbishop Corrigan had been given a house by
the Contessa di Cesnola, an American-born lady whose
husband was Director of the Metropolitan Museum of
Art. The Archbishop himself had invited them to New
York, had promised that they should have the house as an
orphanage. So how could this good priest say that they
had no convent?

Father Morelli could only repeat that, to his positive
knowledge, the house in question was not available to
them. The Archbishop would himself explain everything
in the morning; meanwhile they had best spend the
night in a hotel.

The only hotel they could afford was a rooming-house so filthy that they spent the night sitting in hard chairs rather than trust themselves to the verminous beds or the dirt-encrusted floors. The next day was, as it happened, April the First—but Archbishop Corrigan was plainly in no joking mood.

Frostily he told the sisters that the house offered by the Contessa was unsuitably located and the money which she had provided not enough for their work. He had written them to this effect: apparently they had not received the letter. There was, however, nothing to be done. They had better return to Italy as soon as possible.

Poor Archbishop! He did not know the calibre of the woman who now faced him across his desk, nor did he know what obstacles she had already overcome. Calmly Mother Cabrini spread before him the Vatican documents instructing her, in the Pope's name, to begin work among Italian immigrants in the United States and specifically in the New York archdiocese. Three weeks later the Sisters were welcoming the first orphans to the house which the Contessa had provided.

Archbishop Corrigan had been right about one thing. The Contessa's subsidy, though generous, was not enough to meet their needs. When cash ran out, the sisters went into the streets to beg more—and they got it.

The Archbishop was soon won over: the forbidding frown was seen no longer and in the years that followed he gave the sisters much encouragement and help. His initial iciness was never fully explained, though it appears that a disagreement had soured his relationship with the Contessa and possibly caused him to look less kindly on the project. Also, he genuinely feared that an orphanage for poor Italian children might cause trouble in an area largely occupied by prosperous Protestants.

Begging helped the sisters to get started, and during

the next twenty-eight years, with Mother Cabrini at their
head, they begged their way across America. Not only
orphanages but schools in abundance were founded, and
hospitals named after Columbus, the first Italian immigrant.

As American girls—some of non-Italian origin—came
forward to join the Missionary Sisters, the work spread
beyond Italian communities and beyond the United
States. In Nicaragua, Panama, Argentina and Brazil there
were new foundations. Six times Mother Cabrini re-
crossed the Atlantic, to revisit Italy and to open houses in
England, France and Spain.

The official histories say that the Missionaries of the
Sacred Heart were founded at Codogno, Italy, on November 14, 1880. Really they were founded long before
that, when a little girl in the Lombard village of Sant'
Angelo di Lodi put handfuls of violets into paper boats
and sent them off down the River Adda. Rosa, an unpo-
etic older sister, upbraided her for wasting her time on
such silly sport. The child, whom the family called Cecchina, shook her head. "God will take care of them," she
said. "They are missionaries. They'll go all the way to
China. . . ."

Always a bright child, Cecchina was especially fascinated by geography and would spend hours poring over
maps of far-distant lands. A missionary priest, passing
through her village one day, gave a talk about his work.
From then on, Francesca Maria Cabrini knew where her
future lay.

As she grew up, however, it looked as though Providence had vetoed her ambition to become a nun. The
youngest of a farmer's thirteen children, she qualified as
a schoolteacher with the highest of marks. She was also
extremely devout: she slept on boards and gave all her
free time to prayer and meditation. Yet two Orders to

whom she applied—the Daughters of the Sacred Heart
and the Canossian Sisters—each turned her down on the
ground of insufficient health.

Stern with herself, stern with the children she taught,
Francesca was undermining her constitution with too
much mortification. In time she learned to be gentler
with both herself and her pupils—she had been afraid
that if she let her sunny nature shine through, the
youngsters might take advantage. Eventually, too, she
did become a nun, though few sisters in all history have
had a more bizarre and difficult entry into the religious
life.

Her chance—if chance it can be called—came when
the local pastor asked her to move into the House of
Providence in Codogno. This strange institution, officially an orphanage, was presided over by one Antonia
Toldoni, a wilful and well-to-do woman who frequently
ran short of ready cash because she was always sending
money to a ne'er-do-well nephew. She and the two
women who helped her wore nun-like black dresses,
though no veils, and they had taken certain vows which
they consistently failed to keep. They quarreled constantly, setting a bad example to the children and neglecting them in the process.

Francesca's task was to be temporary; the pastor fondly
imagined that a fortnight or so would suffice to put the
House of Providence into reasonable order. Francesca
realised from the outset that it was going to take very
much longer than that.

Since Antonia was still officially the Superior,
Francesca's position was ambiguous. It swiftly became
almost untenable. For three years she was pushed
around by the tempestuous, unbalanced woman, who
became increasingly jealous as Francesca, in the teeth of
all opposition, turned the orphanage into a happy and

successful home for the children. Young girls began to come to her for spiritual guidance until eventually she had thirty of these quasi-novices to help and advise.

Impressed, both the pastor and the Bishop himself began to treat Francesca as though she, and not Antonia, was the Superior of the house. As Antonia's rage mounted, she subjected the young woman to torrents of abuse and even to physical violence. Had the Bishop known what was happening, he would certainly have acted but Francesca, out of loyalty, kept silent. Finally Antonia signed promissory notes for her nephew which she could not possibly honor. With the House of Providence facing ruin, Francesca was forced to speak.

Bishop Gelmini tried to remove Antonia. She responded with an action against him in the civil court, compelling him to excommunicate her. The House of Providence was dissolved and both orphans and novices sent elsewhere. Francesca was now a nun with neither convent nor Order. At this time she was thirty years old.

To her astonishment and delight, the Bishop suggested that she found an Order of missionary nuns. The need was great, he said, and she was eminently suited to the work. And so the Order was founded, with seven sisters, in a house without chairs, tables or even enough crockery to go round. Now that she was at last a missionary, Francesca added "Saverio" (Xavier) to her baptismal name, in honor of the great Jesuit saint.

To every difficulty—and she faced many—Francesca Saverio Cabrini had one response: "Who is doing this? We, or Our Lord?" More than once, she had to contend with discouragement from high-ranking clerics. Archbishop Corrigan was not the first prelate, or the most senior, to find himself beaten by her quick wit and her persistence. In September, 1887, having established several houses in her native Lombardy, she travelled to Rome to set up a base there. Her first interview with the

Cardinal Vicar was a dismal one. Yes, she might open a new house, he said grudgingly, provided that she had enough capital—and by enough he meant half a million lire.

Cardinal Parrochi must have known that the sisters did not have anything like that sum. He had, in any case, made it fairly clear that he saw no role for them in the Eternal City.

"Wait and see, God will change his heart," Mother Cabrini told her companion as soon as they were outside the door. And off she went to seek approval of her newly-drafted Rule from the Sacred Congregation concerned.

A few days later she asked for a second interview with the Cardinal Vicar. This was granted.

"I don't know what I can say to you that hasn't been said already," Cardinal Parrochi remarked when his visitor had settled herself in a chair.

"If you don't know, Eminence, then perhaps it would be best to ask the Pope," replied Mother Cabrini blithely.

To his own astonishment Cardinal Parrochi found himself promising to do just that. A fortnight later he called her back. Not only would Mother Cabrini be permitted to open a house in the Pope's diocese, she was *commanded* to open two: a school for poor children in the slums of Porta Pia and a kindergarten in a poverty-stricken village called Aspra.

It was not long before Leo XIII sent for this dynamic Mother Cabrini from Lombardy, of whom he had heard so much. This first audience was just a friendly chat about the work which she was doing with her 150 nuns. It was later that he uttered the famous command that sent her to America.

By this time Cardinal Parrochi had become a staunch admirer—a transformation which Archbishop Corrigan

was to repeat later on. The Cardinal Vicar was among
those who were convinced that the Order's work was in
the United States, and he so advised Pope Leo.

Every saint has faults to overcome and Mother Cabrini
had hers. She could be tactless and unbending, especially when faced by lifestyles which she did not understand and which fell short of her own high standards. In
Nicaragua, where she and her sisters were given an enthusiastic welcome, she refused to take her place at a
dinner in her honor until the Indian serving-women
were more adequately attired. In the days that followed
she found much else to shock and displease her.

Whereas the crowds had cheered themselves hoarse
for the sisters' arrival, their critical attitude caused so
much resentment that hostile mobs surrounded the convent, shouting insults and firing guns into the air. A certain anti-Protestant prejudice also marred Mother Cabrini's outlook during her early years in the United States.

Yet a saint she became, despite these blemishes, and
she also fought a constant battle with ill-health. The English language proved a great trial, for she did not possess
the linguistic gift of a John Neumann. Since learning
English was one of the crosses by whose means she
reached sainthood, perhaps she has the best title of all to
be included in this book!

In 1909, at Seattle, Mother Cabrini became a
naturalised American. The outbreak of war in 1914 sad-
dened her deeply, that war in which so many thousands
of young men, including Italians, were daily losing their
lives. When in 1917 her adopted country was also drawn
into the conflict, her sadness was all the greater.

She died as the year drew to a close, one of her last acts
being to wrap Christmas gifts for children under her
care. In 1946 she was canonised by Pope Pius XII—the
first American citizen to be declared a saint.

BIBLIOGRAPHY

Butler's Lives of the Saints, edited by Herbert Thurston, S. J., and Donald Attwater (Burns & Oates, London, 1956).

The Penguin Dictionary of Saints, edited by Donald Attwater (Penguin Books, Harmondsworth, Middlesex, 1978).

Encyclopedia Britannica (Encyclopedia Britannica Inc., Chicago, 1973).

The Golden Days of the Early English Church, by Sir Henry H. Howorth (John Murray, London, 1917).

A History of the English Church and People, by Bede. Translated by Leo Sherley-Price (Penguin Books, Harmondsworth, Middlesex, 1955).

Bede's Ecclesiastical History of the English Nation (Everyman's Library, London, 1970).

St. Hilda of Whitby: Historical Notes, complied by Norman Moorsom (Whitby, 1970)

Companion Guide to the North-East Coast of England, by John Seymour (Collins, London, 1974).

The Life of the Celtic Church, by James Bullock (St. Andrew Press, Edinburgh, 1963).

A Social History of England from 55 B.C. to A.D. 1215, by Ralph Arnold (Constable, London, 1967).

Cuthbert of Lindisfarne, His Life and Times, by A. C. Fryer (Partridge, London, 1880).

185

Two Lives of St. Cuthbert, translated by Bertram Colgrave (Cambridge University Press, 1940).

Anglo-Saxon Saints and Scholars, by E. S. Duckett (Macmillan, New York, 1947).

The Venerable Bede: His Life and Writings, by G. F. Browne (Macmillan, New York, 1919).

Royal Pearl, by A. M. D. Henderson-Howat (SPCK, London, 1948).

Margaret of Scotland, Queen and Saint, by T. Ratcliffe Barnett (Oliver and Boyd, Edinburgh, 1926).

Saint Margaret, Queen of Scotland, by Lucy Menzies (J. M. Dent, London, 1925).

Magna Vita Sancti Hugonis, by Adam, Prior of Eynsham; edited by Decima L. Douie and Hugh Farmer, OSB (Nelson, London, 1961).

St. Hugh of Lincoln, by R. M. Woolley (SPCK, London, 1927).

Hugh, Bishop of Lincoln, by C. L. Marson (Arnold, London, 1901).

Thomas Becket, Archbishop of Canterbury, by W. H. Hutton (Pitman, London, 1910).

Thomas Becket, by Richard Winston (Constable, London, 1967).

Thomas Becket, by David Knowles (A. & C. Black, London, 1971).

Lives of St. Thomas More, by William Roper and Nicholas Harpsfield (Everyman, London, 1963).

The Story of Thomas More, by John Farrow (Collins, London, 1956).

The Field is Won: The Life and Death of St. Thomas More, by E. E. Reynolds (Burns & Oates, London, 1968).

Born For Friendship: The Spirit of St. Thomas More, by Bernard Bassett, SJ (Burns & Oates, London, 1965).

St. Thomas More: Selected Letters, edited by Elizabeth Frances Rogers (Yale University Press, 1961).

Utopia, by Thomas More. Translated by Ralph Robynson (Heritage Press, New York, 1959).

Tower of Martyrs, by Leo Knowles, article in *Catholic Digest,* November, 1978.

Margaret Clitherow, by Mary Claridge (Burns & Oates, London, 1966).

Edmund Campion, by Evelyn Waugh (Longmans Green, London, 1961).

Saint Philip Howard, by Margaret Fitzherbert (Incorporated Catholic Truth Society, London, 1975).

A Martyr Bishop: The Life of Oliver Plunkett, by John McKee (Lumen Christi Press, Houston, Texas, 1975).

The Way of a Martyr, by Martin Bennett (Holy Ghost Books, London, 1973).

The Trial of Oliver Plunkett, by Alice Curtayne (Sheed and Ward, London, 1953).

Mrs. Seton: Foundress of the American Sisters of Charity, by J. I. Dirvin, CM (Farrar, Straus & Giroux, New York, 1975).

Elizabeth Seton, An American Woman, by Leonard Feeney, SJ (America Press, New York, 1938).

Autobiography, by St. John Neumann (St. Paul Editions, Boston, Mass., 1977).

Blessed John Neumann: The Helper of the Afflicted, by W. Frean, CSSR (Majellan Press, Ballarat, Australia, 1963).

Blessed John Neumann, Bishop of Philadelphia, by J. J. Galvin, CSSR (Helicon, Baltimore, 1964).

Harvester of Souls: John Neumann, by Tom Langan (Our Sunday Visitor, Huntington, Indiana, 1977).

Mother Francesca Saverio Cabrini, by C. C. Martindale, SJ (Burns, Oates & Washbourne, London, 1931).

Mother Cabrini, Missionary to the World, by Frances Parkinson Keyes (Vision Books, New York, 1959).